# Raising Godly Kids in the 21<sup>st</sup> Century

I0111412

By Rev. Armand Prentiss

© 2015

Unless otherwise notated, all scriptures in this book are taken from the New King James Version®. Copyright © 1982 by Thomas Nelson. Used by permission. All rights reserved.

THE HOLY BIBLE, NEW INTERNATIONAL VERSION®, NIV® Copyright © 1973, 1978, 1984, 2011 by Biblica, Inc.™ Used by permission. All rights reserved worldwide. These Scriptures are copyrighted by the Biblica, Inc.™

Scripture quotations marked (NLT) are taken from the *Holy Bible*, New Living Translation, copyright ©1996, 2004, 2007, 2013 by Tyndale House Foundation. Used by permission of Tyndale House Publishers, Inc., Carol Stream, Illinois 60188. All rights reserved.

Scripture quotations marked (JBP) are taken from "The New Testament in Modern English", 1962 edition, published by HarperCollins.

Dedicated to the Lord Jesus Christ, my incredible parents, Armand and June Prentiss, and the best wife ever, Lonie. I also dedicate this work to my children, Grace, Evan, Anne, and David, who were the guinea pigs for the learning experiences that became this book.

All profits from this book will be donated to taking care of orphans in developing nations.

# ACKNOWLEDGEMENTS

I would like to acknowledge my pastor, Rev. Paul Neel, who has been my partner for much of my child rearing years. We have been there for each other through the good times and the bad.

Also I want to recognize the congregation of Assembly Christian Center of New Iberia, who have allowed me to teach the Word of God. Believe me, you have taught me more than I have taught you! Also, a great "Thank you!" to Mitchell Prudhomme for his help in bringing this book to press.

# TABLE OF CONTENTS

"When my kids become wild and unruly, I use a nice, safe playpen. When they're finished, I climb out."
-Erma Bombeck

# FORWARD

In Nehemiah 13, we read, "*In those days I also saw Jews who had married women of Ashdod, Ammon, and Moab. And half of their children spoke the language of Ashdod, and could not speak the language of Judah, but spoke according to the language of one or the other people.*" (NKJV)

In our day this has become true even in the homes of Christian parents. Our progeny speak the language of the world- its culture, values, quotes and songs of celebrities, and do not speak the language of God. In short, the next generation is being stolen out from under our care!

**The purpose of this book is not to replace the amazing parenting books on the market**. (James Dobson will not need to lose sleep!). But in the 35 years I have been working with young people, I have found some truths and strategies I do not see readily available in the resources on the bookshelves. It is for this purpose that I am publishing this work.

It is vital that the current situation is altered. As the Lord states in Malachi 4:6, *"And he will turn the hearts of the fathers to the children, and the hearts of the children to their fathers, lest I come and strike the earth with a curse."* (NKJV)

One more thing: it is only by the grace of our wonderful Father that we can be the mothers and fathers we are called to be. No one has a "magic formula," or "Nine Keys to Wonderful Kids," or any other guarantee to success in child-rearing. As the Lord told Ahaz, **"If you do not stand firm in your faith, you will not stand at all."**

# INTRODUCTION

## Sarah's Story

I first met Sarah when I was the new youth pastor of a church. She was 14 years old, and came from a very dysfunctional home. I would notice her hand trembling when she went to open the door of her house- she did not know what was awaiting her on the other side. As things went from bad to worse at home, Sarah began staying with my wife and me more and more. Eventually she moved in with us and stayed several years. Out of this terrible upbringing, she was able to rise up and become a wife and the mother of some great children of her own. As a medical professional, she has had a phenomenal opportunity to share her life with others from broken, abusive homes. This is what the grace of God can do!

**A word before we start:**

In this work you will see strategies and suggestions for how to have a great relationship with your child, and see them serve the Lord. If you hear something that causes you pain, as you realize you erred in your attempt at ministering to your child, I encourage you to learn and let it go. I know parents of grown children who get depressed wondering if they had done some minor thing differently when their child was small, if it would have changed the current situation. This is very negative and useless. Evaluate the present and plan for the future! The past is only good for learning for the next challenge. As it says in Rom. 15:4, *"For whatever things were written before were written for our learning, that we through the patience and comfort of the Scriptures might have hope."* (NKJV)

## A. Two mistakes I am making teaching this series:

1. You never teach on something someone can observe in your personal life. One person said the definition of an expert is someone who is more than 50 miles from home! While I have tried to raise my four children by the principles in this book (as I have discovered them), I certainly have often failed in executing them (the principles- I've never executed any of the children!) every time. This does not point to the information as being wrong (since most if not all the material is from Scripture), but that the parent failed in applying them. Having acknowledged my shortcomings, I will say that so far my children are turning out pretty well, and by the Grace of our Lord will be mighty for His Kingdom. Psalms 127:4-5 says, "*Like arrows in the hand of a warrior, so are the children of one's youth. Happy is the man who has his quiver full of them; they shall not be ashamed...*"

2.  I have shortcomings in my responses to my children, most notably getting irritated quickly over small things that do not matter. This is sin, when Eph. 6:4 is applied, *"And you, fathers, do not provoke your children to wrath, but bring them up in the training and admonition of the Lord."* Also, Titus 1:7, *"...not quick-tempered..."*

My children are all either married, in their careers, or in college, so the child-training phase of our lives is over. Now, we get to sit and watch our children avoid the mistakes we made, while probably making new ones of their own.

B. **Before getting down on your ability as a parent, remember you could always do worse. Check out this verse:**
Lk. 2:41-43

> *"His parents went to Jerusalem every year at the Feast of Passover.  And when He was twelve years old, they went up to Jerusalem according to the custom of the feast.  When*

they had finished the days, as they returned, the Boy Jesus lingered behind in Jerusalem. And Joseph and His mother did not know it; but supposing Him to have been in the company, they went a day's journey, and sought Him among their relatives and acquaintances.  So when they did not find Him, they returned to Jerusalem, seeking Him." (NKJV)

So, the next time you feel like a failure at parenting, remember that God trusted Joseph and Mary with His Only Son, and they misplaced Him!

C. **We are going to look at building Godly kids like building a house**.
The analogy will not be perfect, but may help in remembering the different components to successfully raising children who are a blessing to their family and to the Lord Jesus Christ.

# CHAPTER ONE:

# THE "THEME" OF THE HOUSE

**The "theme of the house:**

Different houses have different themes: Ranch, Mediterranean, Acadian, etc. What is the theme of our child?

- We do not want our children to be well behaved, or "good," or popular, or any other positive attribute. These emphases are often based on our selfish desire for our children to make us look good. Our children can possess all of these and still miss heaven! What we want is for each child to take on the nature of Christ, to be like Jesus. It is our carnal nature that wants our children to "look good" in front of others. **We need to place priority on our children looking good to God.**

## Training a Child in the Way He (or she) Should Go

In Prov. 22:6 it states, "*Train up a child in the way he should go, and when he is old he will not depart from it.*" There are some keys to "laying out the design" of our child found in this verse:

a. The training assumes an active role on the part of the parents. That is assumed in the text. Love, knowledge (civic, familial, vocational, and spiritual), wisdom (correct application of knowledge), encouragement, and discipline are all part of the process involved in the training of a child "in the way he should go."

b. Another important point is made by James Dobson, who points out that the training should reflect the aptitudes, talents, and interests of the child.

c. How many children have been the focal point of a dad who had unfulfilled dreams in sports attempting to live out their fantasies through their offspring? How many times have children participated in activities they had no interest in to please their parents?

d. How many parents have placed unrealistic expectations on their child in music, academics, or other areas for which the child had no gift or aptitude, putting the child in a stressful mindset, with the prospect of failure forcing them to blame others, cheat, or build excuses for their inability to succeed?

In the classic, *The Christian Family*, by Larry Christenson, he writes,

"We are to train up the child not simply in the way that any and every child should go, but also in *the* (specific and unique) way in which *he* should go. This means that parents must deal with each one of their children under the creative leading of the Holy Spirit. All parents have to adjust to the sometimes difficult realization that each one of their children is different...

Parents must be on their guard lest they visit upon a child something of their own desire and ambition. It is not uncommon that a father will try to live out some aspect of his own life through the life of his child...but if his daughter has a different set of sealed orders...it can cause untold suffering and frustration."

While there is no doubt that there are occasions where an activity has merit regardless of the child's interest in it, (learning the basics of music through piano, learning the concept of teamwork through a recreational team sport, etc.), there should be no excessive pressure to be superior in the activity.

On Dobson's website is an observation by Rev. Tommy Nelson, that sums this up this topic well:

> "Our children are created in God's image, not ours. He formed the spirit of our children, not us. They are on loan to us. Our children have to know we love and accept them for who they are. Our children need to know we are excited about how God made them, rather than frustrated about what He didn't make. Let's appreciate our children individually and do whatever it takes to help them develop the unique gifts God gave them within their particular temperament."

# CHAPTER TWO:

# BLUEPRINTS FOR BUILDING GODLY CHILDREN

"Unless the Lord builds the house, its builders labor
in vain."
- Ps. 127:1

## *BLUEPRINTS FOR BUILDING GODLY CHILDREN*

What do our children use as blueprints for building
their lives?

The Bible?  Jesus?  No, our lives.

Prov. 22:6 "Train up a child in the way he should go,
and when he's old he will not depart from it.

How do we do that?  What needs to be in the
blueprints that will prepare our children to live for
Christ?

# BLUEPRINTS

## A. Sowing: Bad, Inconsistent and Good Examples

### 1. Sowing: Bad Examples

#### a. Bad examples of sowing in Scripture:

- Gen. 27:15-23 Jacob tricks his father with an animal skin for flesh, and Jacob's sons trick him with a dead animal.

- I Sam. 2:12, 29 Eli's sons
  I Sam. 8:3 Samuel's sons:  Samuel modeled what he was exposed to.  (These will be examined more closely in subsequent chapters.)

- There are about 15 more of these I have found in Scripture, including Abraham and Isaac, kings of Israel and Judah.  Sowing and reaping will appear in our lives, as well as in our progeny.

## b. Generational Curses:

Deut. 5:9b "*For I, the Lord your God, am a jealous God, visiting the iniquity of the fathers upon the children to the third and fourth generations of those who hate Me.*" (NKJV) This is not a spooky statement. The sins of our ancestors impact our lives.

A close friend of mine had his inheritance lost by a relative who forged family names on a contract to sell out the family business. Instead of owning a share of the business, there was nothing. Why did this happen? Because the relative had a gambling problem. The sins of the previous generation were a curse on his life. This does not mean that we will be judged by God for the sins of our ancestors, though. Look at Eze. 18:4-21 (KJV)

*4 Behold, all souls are mine; as the soul of the father, so also the soul of the son is mine: the soul that sinneth, it shall die.*

⁵ But if a man be just, and do that which is lawful and right,

⁶ And hath not eaten upon the mountains, neither hath lifted up his eyes to the idols of the house of Israel, neither hath defiled his neighbour's wife, neither hath come near to a menstruous woman,

⁷ And hath not oppressed any, but hath restored to the debtor his pledge, hath spoiled none by violence, hath given his bread to the hungry, and hath covered the naked with a garment;

⁸ He that hath not given forth upon usury, neither hath taken any increase, that hath withdrawn his hand from iniquity, hath executed true judgment between man and man,

⁹ Hath walked in my statutes, and hath kept my judgments, to deal truly; he is just, he shall surely live, saith the Lord GOD.

¹⁰ If he beget a son that is a robber, a shedder of blood, and that doeth the like to any one of these things,

¹¹ And that doeth not any of those duties, but even hath eaten upon the mountains, and defiled his neighbour's wife,

¹² Hath oppressed the poor and needy, hath spoiled by violence, hath not restored the pledge, and hath lifted up his eyes to the idols, hath committed abomination,

¹³ Hath given forth upon usury, and hath taken increase: shall he then live? he shall not live: he hath done all these abominations; he shall surely die; his blood shall be upon him.

¹⁴ Now, lo, if he beget a son, that seeth all his father's sins which he hath done, and considereth, and doeth not such like,

¹⁵ That hath not eaten upon the mountains, neither hath lifted up his eyes to the idols of the

house of Israel, hath not defiled his neighbour's wife,

¹⁶ Neither hath oppressed any, hath not withholden the pledge, neither hath spoiled by violence, but hath given his bread to the hungry, and hath covered the naked with a garment,

¹⁷ That hath taken off his hand from the poor, that hath not received usury nor increase, hath executed my judgments, hath walked in my statutes; he shall not die for the iniquity of his father, he shall surely live.

¹⁸ As for his father, because he cruelly oppressed, spoiled his brother by violence, and did that which is not good among his people, lo, even he shall die in his iniquity.

¹⁹ Yet say ye, Why? doth not the son bear the iniquity of the father? When the son hath done that which is lawful and right, and hath kept all my statutes, and hath done them, he shall surely live.

*20 The soul that sinneth, it shall die. The son shall not bear the iniquity of the father, neither shall the father bear the iniquity of the son: the righteousness of the righteous shall be upon him, and the wickedness of the wicked shall be upon him.*

*21 But if the wicked will turn from all his sins that he hath committed, and keep all my statutes, and do that which is lawful and right, he shall surely live, he shall not die.* (KJV)


So we see God says He will not hold the child responsible for the sins of the parent, nor the parent for the sins of the child.  The meaning of Deut. 5 is that the tough conditions caused by rebellion to the Lord influence the children and grandchildren.  Of course, if the cycle is not broken, the generational curse continues for another generation! I am so thankful to my parents, and their willingness to break curses so that I did not have to face them! Single parent families without dads have become a

27

cause of young men being incarcerated, which is an example of modern generational curses. This is a part of the sowing and reaping (or "planting and harvesting").

Before we get into the principle of sowing and reaping, let's take a moment to pray. "Father, we come to you in the Name above all Names, Jesus Christ. We ask that we would be the generation that breaks the curse of bondage off our lives, that our children need not deal with any generational curses. Help us to turn to you, and receive the strength to overcome life-controlling addictions and habits, in Jesus' Name, Amen.

## c. Bad Examples in Our Personal Lives

Let me present a situation for your consideration. A man wants to grow corn. So, he prepares the soil, insures a stable water supply, fertilizes, and then plants wheat. When he goes out to his garden, he finds that what is growing out of the ground does not look like corn. He is very upset, and complains to his friends that even though he is watering, weeding, and fertilizing, no matter what he does the ground is not yielding for him the crop he desires. A Jewish person might say, "Meshuggener! Why would you plant wheat and expect corn?" And he would be right in his denunciation. **So why do so many of us plant anger, frustration, strife, complaining, and criticism but expect to harvest love, peace and joy in the Holy Spirit**? Are we less irrational than the deluded farmer? One warning regarding this is found in Pr. 14:1, *"The wise woman builds her house, but the foolish pulls it down with her hands."* (NKJV) Would it not be a terrible indictment to find the source of the failure of God's spirit to work in our family was due to our consistent negativism toward our parents, our children, our spouse? Scripture is clear:" Do not be deceived, God is not mocked; for whatever a man sows, that he will also reap." (Gal. 6:7 NKJV))

2. **Sowing: Inconsistent Examples**:

Compare:

Prov. 4:3  (Solomon speaking) *"When I was my father's son, tender and the only one in the sight of my mother, he also taught me, and said to me: let your heart retain my words; keep my commands, and live."*

With

I Ki. 1:5-6 *"And his father (David) had not rebuked him at any time by saying, Why have you done so?..."*

David trained one of his kids, the other he never talked to.


3. **Good Consistent Examples**:  II Tim. 1:5-6  "... *when I call to remembrance the genuine faith that is in you, which dwelt first in your grandmother Lois and your mother Eunice, and I am persuaded is in you also."* (NKJV)  \*\***Note to single mothers: the**

**dads are not listed as having had a role in the spiritual development in Timothy's life. You don't have to give up if your husband is not "in the game."** I will cover strategies for single moms later in this volume.

Why aren't we- the people of God- not getting the blessings of God? Hear the words of Hosea: Hos. 10:12 *"Sow for **yourselves** righteousness, reap in mercy."* (NKJV) We can sow blessings, favor, peace and joy into our lives and our families, as easily as sowing judgment, strife and anger.

Other examples would have to do with marriage, handling conflict, priorities in life, etc.

> "For a man to conquer himself is the first and noblest victory." - Dennis Demuth

3. **The Molding of the Will into Obedience to the Holy Spirit.**

There can be no doubt that to manage the child's will and to teach self-control is the essential step in raising a child to follow the leading of the Lord and reject the impulse toward selfishness.

Herbert Spencer stated, "The most important attribute of man as a moral being is the faculty of self-control…There never has been, and cannot be, a good life without self-control; apart from self-control, no good life is imaginable. For a man to conquer himself is the first and noblest victory." (*Spirit Directed Discipline*, Demuth, p. 13)

Susanna Wesley, in her article, "*Conquer the Child's Will,*" points out that the self-will is the key to raising Godly children:

## "Conquer the Child's Will"

"In order to form the minds of children, the first thing to be done is to conquer their will and bring them to an obedient temper. To inform the understanding is a work of time and must with children proceed by slow degrees as they are able to bear it: but the subjecting of the will is a thing which must be done at once; and the sooner the better. For by neglecting timely correction, they will contract a stubbornness and obstinacy which is hardly ever after conquered; and never, without using such severity as would be as painful to me as to the child. In the esteem of the world they pass for kind and indulgent, whom I call cruel, parents, who permit their children to get habits that they know must be afterward broken. Nay, some are so stupidly fond as in sport to teach their children to do things, which, in a while after, they have severely beaten them for doing.

"Whenever a child is corrected, it must be conquered; and this will be no hard matter to do if it be not grown headstrong by too much indulgence. And when the will of a child is totally subdued and it is brought to revere and stand in awe of the parents, then a great many childish follies and inadvertences may be passed by. Some should be overlooked and taken no notice of, and others mildly reproved; but no willful transgression ought ever to be forgiven children without chastisement, less or more, as the nature and circumstances of the offense require.

"I insist upon conquering the will of children betimes, because this is the only strong and rational foundation of a religious education; without which both precept and example will be ineffectual. But when this is thoroughly done, then a child is capable of being governed by the reason and piety of its parents, till its own understanding comes to maturity and the principles of religion have taken root in the mind.

"I cannot yet dismiss this subject. As self-will is the root of all sin and misery, so whatever cherishes this in children insures their after-wretchedness and irreligion; whatever checks and mortifies it promotes their future happiness and piety. This is still more evident if we further consider that religion is nothing else than the doing the will of God and not our own: that the one grand impediment to our temporal and eternal happiness being this self-will, no indulgencies of it can be trivial, no denial unprofitable.

(ccel.org/ccel/Wesley/journal.vi.iv.xx.html?highlight=susanna, wesley#highlight)

Focusing on this makes the incredible failure of King David to contest his son Adonijah's will even more striking:

*"And his father had not rebuked him at any time by saying, 'why have you done so?"* (NKJV)

Or in the NLT, "*Now his father, King David, had never disciplined him at any time, even by asking, 'What are you doing?'*"

## The Role of the parent

As the Old Testament was our tutor in teaching us God's laws (Gal. 3:25), so the parent is God's means of training children in God's ways. That we are born with a sinful nature is an accepted tenet of the Christian faith. And while some may argue what that entails, anyone who has told a toddler not to touch something, and watched the child edge over, and attempt to touch it without detection, knows there is a desire to violate our ruler's desires for our own. This is covered in Rom. 8:13, "*For if you live according to the flesh you will die; but if by the Spirit you put to death the deeds of the body, you will live.*" (NKJV)

The J.B. Phillips translation gives a little more perspective: "*So then, my brothers, you can see that we owe no duty to our sensual nature, or to live life on the level of the instincts. Indeed that way of living leads to certain spiritual death. But if on the other hand you cut the nerve of your instinctive actions by obeying the Spirit, you will live."*

How do we bring about this change in our child's nature?   While only Jesus Christ can change our kid's nature in this or any other century, we are the agents for changing their assumption that their will is supreme.  A pastor friend of mine was fond of saying, "If you don't make your child cry when they are little, they are going to make you cry when they are big." This will be discussed more in the section on "Correction." Kathie Walters, in her book, *Parenting by the Spirit*, says, "If the children are going to learn to obey God's voice then they must first learn to obey yours." (p.22)  Our desire is for God's will to be the primary source of our child's decisions (Phil. 2:13).

It cannot be overstated how vital the control of the will is in determining success spiritually. Jerry Bridges in "*The Pursuit of Holiness* points out,

"It is the will that ultimately makes each individual choice of whether we will sin or obey.  It is the will that chooses to yield to temptation, or to say no.  Our wills, then, ultimately determine our moral destiny, whether we will be holy or unholy in our character and conduct.

## Can Children Be Self-Governing? Hint: the answer is "No"

I am constantly amazed at the number of parents who allow their children- often as young as elementary- to determine which school they will attend (public, Christian, home-school). The same goes for attendance at Church camps, and church services. A 9 year old does not have the experience, maturity or wisdom to determine what is in their best interest. I realize with a strong-willed child this can make for a battle in the home. The earlier these battles are won, the easier the future will be.

Which flavor of ice cream is fine for decision-making. The potential life-changing experience at a

school, going to church, or Christian retreat is not.
Parents must not waive their obligation before the
Lord to lead!


## SELFISHNESS


The conquering of the will is demonstrated
when selfishness is defeated.  Children, like
adults, want their own way.  When we see
children being selfish, it is our responsibility to rid
their personality of selfishness, in whatever
manifestation it is revealed (greed, having their
own way, refusing to help another, etc.). The
goal is to help our children recognize selfishness,
view as God does- sin- and want to be rid of it as
soon as possible.  One form of selfishness,
coveting, is described in Col. 3:5, *"Therefore put
to death your members which are on the
earth...and covetousness, which idolatry."* (NKJV)
Do our children recognize selfishness and hate
it?  Do **we** recognize selfishness and hate it?  Do

our children hear us demanding our own way, or serving our spouse?  There is no getting around the fact that without positive outside influences, the example we set for our children will be the example they use.

*"These commandments that I give you today are to be upon your hearts. [7] Impress them on your children. Talk about them when you sit at home and when you walk along the road, when you lie down and when you get up. [8] Tie them as symbols on your hands and bind them on your foreheads. [9] Write them on the doorframes of your houses and on your gates."*

- Deut. 6:6-9

## CHAPTER THREE:

# LAYING THE FOUNDATION

*"For no other **foundation** can anyone lay than that which is laid, which is Jesus Christ."* I Cor. 3:11 (NKJV)

## A. Communication

1. **We cannot schedule "quality time."**

   Quality time will be a function of "quantity time."

   "Can I ask you something?" "You know what I was thinking about the other day?" "Dad, why do we say it is wrong to...?"

   - II Tim. 4:2 "Preach the word! Be ready in season and out of season. Convince, rebuke, exhort, with all longsuffering and teaching."

- Prov. 6:6 "And these words which I command you today shall be in your heart. You shall teach them diligently to your children, and shall talk of them when you sit in your house, when you walk by the way, when you lie down, and when you rise up."

As Josh McDowell says in *Right from Wrong*,

"Our children are not adopting our values and morals. They do not share our priorities and perspectives. And we cannot blame the media...society...government...the Supreme Court...the public schools-they are not entrusted with communicating biblical values to our children- we are! We must not expect to change our culture; we must change the way we respond to it. It does no good to bemoan our society; we must control how much we allow it to influence us and our children." (p.48)

- Prov. 25:11 *A word fitly spoken is like apples of gold in settings of silver."* (NKJV) Or *"Timely advice is as lovely as golden apples in a silver basket."* (NLT)
- Prov. 15:23 *"Everyone enjoys a fitting reply; it is wonderful to say the right thing at the right time!"* (NLT)

## 2. "**More is caught than taught**"

Children will do what you say only until a certain age, and then they will do what you do!

- Prov. 20:7 *"The godly walk with integrity; blessed are their children after them."*
- Hasn't every parent cringed when he saw an expression on their child's face that upset him or her, and then he realized he makes the same expression?  Or what mother has not heard her child say something that aggravated her, and then pictured herself saying the same thing to *her* mom?

So what do we want "caught?" This topic could consume many chapters, but a brief sketch might include:

- Loving our spouse.
  Someone once said, "The best thing a man can do for his children is to love their mother." Studies have shown that how the parents interact will have significant impact on the children's future marriage.
- Regular times of prayer.
  We can talk of the importance of our relationship with God, but if the children do not see their parents devoted to prayer, our words will mean little.
- Going to Church
  This is vital to establish God's priority in the family, even more so for the father to lead in bringing the children.
- Management of Finances
  While Christian stewardship of finances is beyond the scope of this book, if

children see borrowing for instant gratification, arguing over money, and other poor examples in this area, it will affect their ability to handle their future income and decision-making in this area.

- Family time- this is covered in more detail under "quality vs. quantity time."
- The surrendering of our will to that of Jesus Christ's, and to those He calls us to serve.

## 3. Time is a function of love.

Here is an experiment: try substituting the word, "time" for the word "love." The beginning of I Cor. 13. "If I have not time, I am tinkling brass, or a clanging symbol." As a parent, if I have time only to give orders to my children and complain, I am truly clanging.

*"Like all parents, my husband and I just do the best we can, and hold our breath, and hope we've set aside enough money to pay for our kids' therapy."*

## B.   "Rules without Relationship lead to Rebellion"

We must be able to tie in the "rules" to relationship with the Lord, and with our families. Foundation must be built upon Christ.  *"For no other foundation can anyone lay than that which is laid, which is Jesus Christ."* (I Cor. 3:11)  I have seen a teen boy bow up to those in authority, then immediately submit to a different authority called in to correct him. Why the submission to one and not the other? The second teacher had an on going relationship with the child. He knew he was appreciated and valued by the second teacher. Though the first one may have cared, the student did not see a legitimate role of command. Simply put, while perhaps in the past children accepted authoritative roles over their lives, many of them now do not. Today the right to speak correction is earned by showing there is care. The old axiom is, "they won't care how much you know until they know how much you care."

Rules that are not connected to the minor's reality is like memorizing historical facts with no framework. This is useless teaching in history, and is about the same value as a framework for living.

So what if one connects the dots? If we show the rules, or precepts, in the total picture of living a Christian life, the child grasps the overview of being godly.

**Teaching the precepts as characteristics of Christ:**

In Josh McDowell's book *Right from Wrong*, he talks about the "Test of Truth." Without going into great detail, it is important to teach godly rules in relation to the character of the Lord. A few examples:

Precept:    Do not lie, steal, or cheat."

Principle:    Honesty
Person:       God is true

Precept: What God has joined together, let not man separate:

Principle: Unity
Person: God is One

Precept: Do unto others as you would have them do to you."

Principle: Justice
Person: God is just.

## Correcting Children

This is a hard one: when to correct our children? How much? How often? Mom or dad?

## Ignoring Correction

The scriptural admonition of staying within God's boundaries is clear from the passage in Matt. 7:21-23

*Not everyone who says to Me, '"Lord; Lord," shall enter the kingdom of heaven, but he who does the will of My Father in heaven. Many will say to Me in that day, "Lord, Lord, have we not prophesied in Your name, cast out demons in Your name, and done many wonders in Your name?" And then I will declare to them, " I never knew you; depart from Me, you who practice lawlessness!"* (NKJV)

The word in Greek for "lawlessness" is *anomia*, which means "not in the law," or "without law." To place this in a sports analogy: a basketball player makes an amazing 40 foot shot at the buzzer to win the game for his team, and the crowd goes wild. Then they notice the referee running up the sideline waving his hands over his head. "No bucket! No bucket! His foot was out of bounds!" The person who "does for God" but does not stay in God's boundaries is told to depart. Correction to keep our progeny "in bounds" is not important; it is vital.

The Bible is littered with examples of parents who simply refused to correct their children. These two incidents are tragic:

### 1. Eli

*Now the sons of Eli were corrupt; they did not know the Lord...Therefore the sin of the young men was very great before the Lord, for men abhorred the offering of the Lord...Then a man of God came to Eli and said to him, "Thus says the Lord...'Why do you kick at My sacrifice and My offering which I have commanded in My dwelling place, and honor your sons more than Me, to make yourselves fat with the best of all the offerings of Israel My people... In that day I will perform against Eli all that I have spoken concerning his house, from beginning to end. For I have told him that I will judge his house forever* for the iniquity which he knows, **because his sons made themselves vile, and he did not restrain them."** *(I Sam. 2:12-3:14)*

### 2. David

Then Adonijah the son of Haggith exalted himself, saying, "I will be king"; and he prepared for himself chariots and horsemen, and fifty men to run before him. (And his father had not rebuked him at any time by saying, "Why have you done so?" (I Ki. 5-6) In other words, David had never even asked his son, "What are you doing?"

Prov. 29:15 says, *"The rod and rebuke give wisdom, but a child left to himself brings shame to his mother."* (NKJV) These two examples prove the truth to this statement.

### Responding with Correction

When our children behave badly, there are three possible responses:

1. We cannot give enough correction, or too little correction, resulting in the lesson not being learned.

2. We can correct too harshly, resulting in "provoking our children to wrath." (Eph. 6:4)

3. We can administer the right range of correction, where the lesson is learned, and the child is trained to behave correctly in the future. (Even if the immediate response is not positive to correction!)

Let's take a look at each of these in Scripture:

### 1. **Too little correction**:

*Now there was a man from the mountains of Ephraim, whose name was Micah. And he said to his mother, "The eleven hundred shekels of silver that were taken from you, and on which you put a curse, even saying it in my ears- here is the silver with me; I took it." And his mother said, "May you be blessed by the Lord, my son!" so when he had returned the eleven hundred shekels of silver to his mother, his mother said, "*

*I had wholly dedicated the silver from my hand to the Lord from my son, to make a carved image and a molded image; now therefore, I will return it to you." Thus he returned the silver to his mother. Then his mother took two hundred shekels of silver and gave them to the silversmith, and he made it into a carved image and a molded image; and they were in the house of Micah. (Judges 17:1-4)* (NKJV)

Micah's mother had cursed the person who stole her money, not realizing it was her adult son. When Micah confesses, his mother blesses him and gives him part of the silver to create an idol for Micah to keep in his house! What is the penalty for his theft? A reward of two hundred silver pieces! How interesting that after Micah takes the image and appoints one of his sons as priests, the scripture says, *"In those days there was no king in Israel; everyone did what was right in his own eyes."* (Judges 17:6) (NKJV)

Those who are mercy-oriented are going to find no fault with Micah's mother. However, while there are times when mercy is appropriate, mercy given without consequences can lead to an expectancy of life with no penalties for wrongdoing.

"Our youth now love luxury. They have bad manners, contempt for authority; they show disrespect for their elders and love chatter in place of exercise; they no longer rise when elders enter the room; they contradict their parents, chatter before company; gobble up their food and tyrannize their teachers."

- Socrates

## 2. Too much correction:

*And the men of Israel were distressed that day, for Saul had placed the people under oath, saying, "Cursed is the man who eats any food until evening, before I have taken vengeance on my enemies." So none of the people tasted food. Now all the people of the land came to a forest; and there was honey on the ground. And when the people had come into the woods, there was the honey, dripping; but no one put his hand to his mouth, for the people feared the oath.* **But Jonathan had not heard his father charge the people with the oath;** *therefore he stretched out the end of the rod that was in his hand and dipped it in a honeycomb, and put his hand to his mouth; and his countenance brightened...Then Saul said to Jonathan, "Tell me what you have done." And Jonathan told him, and said, I only tasted a little honey with the end of the rod that was in my hand. So now I must die!" Saul answered and said, "God do so and more also; for you shall surely die, Jonathan." (I Sam. 14: 24-44 Bold print added)*

Was Saul excessive in his discipline? He had not announced the death of anyone breaking the fast, only that a curse would be on them. If discipline is to be redemptive, how can capital punishment for a minor crime be beneficial? **When we discipline, the amount of punishment must make sense relative to the offense.**

## 3. God's correction

"It happened in the spring of the year, at the time when kings go out to battle, that David sent Joab and his servants with him, and all Israel; and they destroyed the people of Ammon and besieged Rabbah.  But David remained at Jerusalem.  Then it happened one evening that David arose from his bed and walked on the roof of the king's house.  And from the roof he saw a woman bathing, and the woman was very beautiful to behold. So David sent and inquired about the woman.  And someone said, "Is this not Bathsheba, the daughter of Eliam, the wife of Uriah the Hittite? "Then David sent messengers, and took her; and she came to him, and he lay with her, for she was cleansed from her impurity; and she returned to her house. And the woman conceived; so she sent and told David, and said, "I am with child." In the morning it happened that David wrote a letter to Joab and sent it by the hand of Uriah.  And he wrote in the letter, saying, "Set Uriah in the forefront of the hottest

*battle, and retreat from him, that he may be*
*struck down and die." ... (II Sam. 11:1-15)*

Look at the Lord's discipline.  It makes one wince:

*Why have you despised the commandment of*
*the Lord, to do evil in His sight?  You have killed*
*Uriah the Hittite with the sword; you have taken*
*his wife to be your wife, and have killed him with*
*the sword of the people of Ammon.  Now*
*therefore, the sword shall never depart from your*
*house, because you have despised Me, and have*
*taken the wife of Uriah the Hittite to be your wife*
*.Thus says the Lord: 'Behold, I will raise up*
*adversity against you from your own house; and*
*I will take your wives before your eyes and give*
*them to your neighbor, and he shall lie with your*
*wives in the sight of this sun.  For you did it*
*secretly, but I will do this thing before all Israel,*
*before the sun." So David said to Nathan, "I have*
*sinned against the Lord."  And Nathan said to*
*David, "The Lord also has put away your sin; you*
*shall not die.  However, because by this deed you*
*have given great occasion to the enemies of the*

*Lord to blaspheme, the child also who is born to you shall surely die."* (II Sam. 12:9-14) NKJV)

Does this sound too severe? **David is forgiven his sin, but the consequences of his sin remain.** We must remember that a teenage girl who is pregnant may come to an altar and be saved and forgiven, but she returns to her seat still pregnant. There will still be many hard decisions and tears, though she is as redeemed as the pastor who leads in prayer.

How do we know if the punishment is too harsh? **The result in the child's life will reveal it.** David saw his punishment as just, and walked in the blessings of God afterward.

### Matching the Correction to the Child

Unfortunately there is no "correct" way to discipline a child. The personality of each child is different, as most people with large families can attest. I have children that will repent with only a simple word of disapproval. Others must be punished more forcefully because they are strong willed.  Dr. James Dobson has written much on the strong-willed child, and his resources are readily available.  It need only be said that correction must result in repentance, and the parent's love must always be felt by the child.


### Matching the Correction to the Offense

**Willful disobedience** is a different level of offense to a **spontaneous occurrence** that is not premeditated.  Neither of these are the same as **an accidental act** due to immaturity.  For example, playing in the house might be allowed, and a lamp gets broken during the activity.  This is not disobedience, merely immaturity, and would obviously be different from lashing out at a lamp in anger.  Let's look at these three incidents and what correction might be appropriate:

1.  An accidental act: James was 12 years old, and had mowed the yard once or twice before. His dad told him to go mow, and James said

okay and headed out.  Once he had the mower, and tried to start it, he found it had no gasoline.  Going to the shed, he pulled out the gas tank and poured in the gas.  The mower still did not start.  He had poured in a gas/oil mix used for the weed eater.  His father was very upset with him and made him feel stupid and useless.  This was an inappropriate punishment for an obvious accident, due to immaturity.

2.  A spontaneous act: There would not be enough time to give all the times teachers have witnessed children flair up over little or nothing, and behaved in ways that were wrong.  When our children do this, we need to ask if this is the result of their carnal nature wanting it's way, or if we have "provoked our children to wrath." (Eph. 6:4)  There must be punishment for the behavior, but if we need to apologize for our part, we should do so.

3.  A premeditated act:

*"But those who brazenly violate the Lord's will, whether native Israelites or foreigners blaspheme the Lord, and they must be cut off from the community. Since they have treated the Lord's word with contempt and deliberately disobeyed his commands, they must be completely cut off and suffer the consequences of their guilt."* (Nu. 15:30-31)

The intentional, premeditated act of sin was not forgivable in the Old Testament by any number of sacrifices. This adds new light to David's confession of his sin with Bathsheba and Uriah in

Ps. 51:16-17

*"For you do not desire sacrifice, or else I would give it; You do not delight in burnt offering. The sacrifices of God are a broken spirit and a contrite heart..."*

Obviously, a planned, willful act of disobedience is more serious, and must be dealt with more severely. As Watchman Nee points out in his book, *Spiritual Authority*,

> "Sin is a matter of conduct, but rebellion is a matter of principle. Sin is an act against God's holiness, but rebellion is a principle, standing against God's authority. Therefore, rebellion is much worse." (p.11)

Something to think about: If a child is severely punished for an accident or a spontaneous decision, what is going to be left to do when there is willful rebellion?

## Matching the correction to <u>our</u> personality

A couple came to see me a while back to address the way the dad was punishing the children. She saw him as too harsh in his discipline. Usually in a marriage one of the parents is more law oriented (often the dad), and the other is mercy oriented (yeah, that is usually the wife). This means there can be a very different idea of what the appropriate punishment should entail. If you ever are in doubt, or in a disagreement, just call me. (Note- I was being polite. Really, don't call me). Biblically, the father is the one who must set the boundaries, and enforce them. He should listen to his wife, if she feels penalties are too harsh, or thinks a different method should be considered. **The wife should have veto authority over the level of anger that father has when he is spanking or correcting the children.** Sir, if she says you are too angry, you are too angry. Take a walk, go outside and shoot free throws, do something- but don't go into your child's presence with personal anger as your motive for discipline! All dialogues between parents regarding child discipline should be done out of earshot of the children! Our Father in heaven holds the dad accountable for the raising of the children. The man who doesn't listen to his wife for input on this is crazy. As men, we don't like being second-guessed. But the most important thing is that the children see a united front.

"Because I said so, that's why."

-Every Parent Whoever Lived

# CHAPTER FOUR:

## WALLS

*"But it so happened, when Sanballat heard that we were rebuilding the wall, that he was furious and very indignant, and mocked the Jews."*

-Nehemiah 4:1

When my wife and I lived in Mexico, our house was fairly secure against intruders, but not from pests. We had a large hole in the bathroom to the outside, and had "guests" come in regularly. Mice came through the hole, snakes through the large gap between the floor and the door, and a couple of scorpions however they wanted! But the most memorable of our visitors was the large iguana that my wife trapped with a basket on the wall. Getting it from the basket in the bedroom to the outside was an unusually exciting adventure.  It was after that day that we decided whatever had to be done to block passage into the house through that hole was going to be done.  No more gaps in the wall!

**Walls are designed to keep out things that would annoy, threaten or negatively affect our family or home.** Burglars could steal our valuables or threaten our safety.  Pests could bite, or damage our food and belongings.  The weather could destroy furnishings and make us very uncomfortable.  Walls are to protect us all the time; against forces we would never welcome into our house.

**In our spiritual lives, and those of our children, we want our walls to keep out worldly thoughts, secular lifestyles, and anything else that can dilute the emphasis on the Spirit or pollute the sanctity of our hearts.**

The book of Nehemiah is the story of the cupbearer of the king of Persia.  Knowing there is no protection of the city, we find the author attempting to rebuild the walls around Jerusalem to protect the temple that had recently been completed under Ezra. When we give our lives to the Lord, scripture says we become a temple of God's Spirit (I Cor. 6:19). Nehemiah's attempt to build a wall protecting the temple is an example of our responsibility to build a wall around our temple, that is, our life. The importance of building a sound wall is voiced in Nehemiah's clarion call: *"Remember the Lord, great and awesome, and fight for your brethren, your sons, your daughters, your wives, and your houses."* -Neh. 4:14 (NKJV) There was no doubt in Nehemiah's mind what was at stake, and there should be none in ours. Our family's spiritual lives are hanging on our dedication to erect barriers against the enemy of our souls. What are some of the attacks Satan will use to destroy our children? A few points from Nehemiah's obstacles and success can help us see the parallels:

1. Neh. 2:19

*"But when Sanballat the Horonite, Tobiah the Ammonite official, and Geshem the Arab heard of it, they laughed at us and despised us, and said, 'What is thing that your are doing?'"* (NKJV)

One obstacle we will face is others telling us that it is ridiculous to erect barriers against the world's influences. "I cannot believe you don't let your children go to…," "What do you mean your family is not allowed to watch…" "You go to church *how often?*" Ridicule is very hard to take, and can cause us to doubt our rules and decisions. The answer is found in the next verse: *The God of heaven Himself will prosper us; therefore we His servants will arise and build, but you have no heritage or right or memorial in Jerusalem."* The fact is no one outside the Kingdom of God has a right to criticize your protection of your family.

2. Neh. 4:3

*"Now Tobiah the Ammonite was beside him, and he said, 'Whatever they build, if even a fox goes up on it, he will break down their stone wall.'"* (NKJV)

If ridicule does not stop us from building the wall, then making us doubt its value will be tried. "Your wall is not strong enough to work," can put fear in our hearts. But God is the strength of our protection, and He wants to replace fear with faith!

3. Neh. 4:7-9

*"Now it happened, when Sanballat, Tobiah, the Arabs, the Ammonites, and the Ashdodites heard that the walls of Jerusalem were being restored and the gaps were beginning to be closed, that they became very angry, and all of them conspired together to come and attack Jerusalem and create confusion."* (NKJV)

When ridicule and doubt did not stop the progress of defense, the outsiders planned open attack, for the purpose of creating confusion.  The Israelites response is a great lesson for us:

*"Nevertheless we make our prayer to our God, and because of them we set a watch against them day and night."*  This is remedy for defeating our enemy, to pray and watch day and night.

4. Neh. 6:1-2

*"Now it happened when...the rest of our enemies heard that I had rebuilt the wall, and that there were no breaks left in it, "though at that time I had not hung the doors in the gates), that Sanballat and Geshem sent to me saying, 'Come, let us meet together among the villages in the plain of Ono.'  But they thought to do me harm."'* (NKJV)

When the walls were finished, the enemy invites Nehemiah to voluntarily step out from behind the security of the walls, so they can have occasion to attack. The invitation to go outside of the walls of Jerusalem is equivalent to compromising. "I see your standards and provision for safety in your family, but why not just temporarily come out, just to talk. Be reasonable!" When we are invited to step out from our spiritual walls as a family to go to Ono, we need to say, "Oh, no!"

5. Neh. 4:10

*"Then Judah said, 'The strength of the laborers is failing, and there is* **so much rubbish** *that we are not able to build the wall."* (NKJV)

This is so applicable to the situation we face in trying to defend our home spiritually. The rubbish represents baggage we have in our lives that inhibits our ability to fortify our spiritual growth.  Our backgrounds, broken marriages with stepparents, mistakes from our youth, not having protected our children when they were younger, only to now deal with their appetites for those things that are destructive. This is why the "strength of the laborers was failing."  It is difficult to overcome past mistakes now that we see what must be done. But Nehemiah was **rebuilding** the walls, walls that had been destroyed for past sin, past mistakes, and past failures.  Nevertheless, he was called by the Lord and empowered by the Holy Spirit to accomplish all the Lord had for him.

## What did Nehemiah do about it?

Interspersed in the obstacles Nehemiah faced in building the wall were the positive steps Nehemiah took to counter the enemy. Let's look at a few of them:

a. Neh. 3:1

"...*Then Eliashib the high priest rose up with his brothers the priests and built the Sheep Gate; they consecrated it and hung its door....*" (NKJV)

The first thing we see is that the beginning of the work was consecrated to the Lord. We really need to give to the Lord our efforts in our homes and our children to the leading and favor of the Lord!

b. Neh. 4:6

"*The people had a mind to work...*" (NKJV)

Protecting our children from society's influence is <u>work</u>! And that is true all the time, so we must have a "mind to work."

c. Neh. 4: 13

"*I set the people according to their families...*"

The family is the foundational unit in the church. Families working in each home, and then working together, constitute a strong force!

d. Neh. 4:14

*"Do not be afraid of them. Remember the Lord, great and awesome, and fight for your brethren, our sons, your daughters, your wives, and your houses."*

We cannot lose hope due to fear! Remember we have the Lord on our side, and His side wins!

e. Neh. 5:10

*"... stop this charging of interest!"*

It is far beyond the scope of this work to delve into family finances. There are many resources, such as Dave Ramsey, that can help you. I will just highlight that one of the steps Nehemiah took to bring God's favor on their enterprise was to honor the

Lord with their finances. The Lord had specifically told them not to charge interest on their fellow Jews. This had to stop, in Nehemiah's opinion, to keep the blessing of God. Financial problems affect marriages, which affects the children.

f. Other observations from Nehemiah's Building of the Wall:

Neh. 3:12

"...*Shallum the son of Hallohesh, leader of half the district of Jerusalem; he and his daughters made repairs*"

Entire families shared in the construction in Jerusalem, and for our homes to be secure everyone must share responsibility. It is essential that the mother and father are "on the same page" when it comes to sanctifying the home. If necessary, there should be pastoral counseling to find unity on the basics of what influences will be permitted.

- Neh. 3:5 "*...but their nobles did not put their shoulders to the work of their Lord.*" It is a dangerous position to believe that we are above the need of sanctification in our homes. How many ministers have fallen, or their children have been overcome in sin, that might have been avoided if more care had been given to outside influences. I Cor. 10:12 states, "*therefore let him who thinks he stands take heed lest he fall.*"

## The three sources of evil influence

The three sources of evil influence are mentioned in scripture: I Jn. 2:16 "*For all that is in the world- the lust of the flesh, the lust of* the eyes, and the pride of life- is not of the Father but is of the world." We see this lived out in Gen. 3:6, "So when the woman saw that the tree was good for food, that it was pleasant to the eyes, and a tree desirable to make one wise, she took of its fruit and ate...."

- "The world" is not referring to the physical, natural world, but to the operating system in society, which is under the control of the devil.

- "The lust of the flesh" means those things which appeal to our "lower animal nature" (Jamison, Fausset, Brown), wanting us to satisfy basic instincts. Instinctive desires are not necessarily evil, but must be submitted to the Lord. Rom. 8:13 says, "So then, my brothers, you can see that we owe no duty to our sensual nature, or to live life on the level of the instincts. Indeed that way of living leads to certain spiritual death. But if on the other hand you cut the nerve of your *instinctive actions by obeying the Sprit, you will live."*

- "The lust of the eyes" would include those things that arouse passion in us, coveting riches or any other thing that makes us discontent with what we have. I Tim. 6:6-10 says,

*"Now godliness with contentment is great gain. For we brought nothing into this world, and it is certain we can carry nothing out. And having food and clothing, with these we shall be content. But those who desire to be rich fall into temptation and a snare, and into many foolish and harmful lusts which drown men in destruction and perdition. For the love of money is a root of all kinds of evil, for which some have strayed from the faith in their greediness, and pierced themselves through with many sorrows."*

- "The pride of life," literally "arrogant assumption," would include ambition and particularly pride. Pride was Satan's source of falling, and is what he used on Jesus in the desert.

These three roots of temptation is what must be guarded against in setting up our walls for our children and our home

## Extra-Biblical Rules

*Family rules not clearly found in Scripture:*
*Rechabites! Jer. 35: 1-19*

Once my wife and I brought our children to a vacation spot that was secular, but where a lot of other Christian families were vacationing, as well. The family was really pumped up. We had never taken this kind of vacation. The excitement had been building for a few weeks prior to the trip. The activities included functions that would be refused by almost all devout Christians, and some activities that would be "questionable." As the week continued, people we had met who professed to be Christians (and I am sure they were) participated in the programs which Lonie and I would not think of joining, as well as some we were not sure about. Our kids observed who was doing what, and questioned why they were not allowed. What to tell them? *"Well, honey, I know the Jones go to church and are friends of ours, but they are going to hell."* Not exactly an option to tell our children!

As the days went by, it became obvious I was going to need to deal with the situation in a way that was overarching, and would settle the controversies not only for this week, but into the future, as well.

I called my family, the Prentiss family, and laid out the policy that would guide our tribe for the future. I explained that the Christians we had met were friends, and we love them. They love the Lord, and are trying to honor God to the best of their ability. (I was assuming this to be the case, and believe it was accurate, for the most part). I then laid out the Prentiss doctrine, which would be our rule of law for the ensuing years:

As the Prentiss family, we live to a standard of holiness that excludes certain activities not specifically prohibited in Scripture. **It is important to note we do not shy away from the term, "holiness."** In modern Christianity the concept appears to be a forbidden word. I do not want to be guilty of legalism, but I do want to be holy before the Lord. Without holiness no one shall see the Lord- it must be pretty important. To me, a simple explanation of this comes from a dear friend, who once said, *"I don't want to do anything that could damage my anointing or my witness."* I have read a lot of books, and heard many sermons, but that is about the best definition of holiness I have heard.

I did not attempt to "sell" the family that our rules were from the Bible. Phillip Yancy in his book, What's so Great about Grace? discusses his frustration with Christian schools and colleges attempting to force extra-biblical rules into the Scriptures:

"I seethed at their contorted attempts to condemn long hair on men, aware that Jesus and most of the biblical characters we studied probably had longer hair than ours and facial hair to boot. The rule about hair length had more to do with the likelihood of offending supporters than with anything in Scripture, but no one dared admit it.

I could not find one word in the Bible about rock music, skirt length…yet authorities in that school made a determined effort to present all these rules as part of the gospel. I was determined not to fall into that trap."

The family rules were *our rules.* No one else's. **We had no right to push on others our rules; neither did we have to defend our family rules to others.** No explanation is required from Scripture to defend this concept. As will be shown in a moment, the existence of a set of family guidelines that are not biblical prohibitions is not only permitted, but is praised.

Family rules join traditions, trips, and other activities to form a bond in our household.

When building a house or office building, the foundation sets the stage for the rest of the building. Regarding children, we must establish the boundaries and rules that will be required for godly children **in our family.** The biblical precedent for this is found in Jer. 35:1-19

> The word which came unto Jeremiah from the LORD in the days of Jehoiakim the son of Josiah king of Judah, saying,
> 2Go unto the house of the Rechabites, and speak unto them, and bring them into the house of the LORD, into one of the chambers, and give them wine to drink.
> 3Then I took Jaazaniah the son of Jeremiah, the son of Habaziniah, and his brethren, and all his sons, and the whole house of the Rechabites;

4And I brought them into the house of the LORD, into the chamber of the sons of Hanan, the son of Igdaliah, a man of God, which was by the chamber of the princes, which was above the chamber of Maaseiah the son of Shallum, the keeper of the door: 5And I set before the sons of the house of the Rechabites pots full of wine, and cups, and I said unto them, Drink ye wine.

6But they said, We will drink no wine: for Jonadab the son of Rechab our father commanded us, saying, Ye shall drink no wine, neither ye, nor your sons forever:

7Neither shall ye build house, nor sow seed, nor plant vineyard, nor have any: but all your days ye shall dwell in tents; that ye may live many days in the land where ye be strangers.

8Thus have we obeyed the voice of Jonadab the son of Rechab our father in all that he hath charged us, to drink no wine all our days, we, our wives, our sons, nor our daughters;

9Nor to build houses for us to dwell in: neither have we vineyard, nor field, nor seed:

¹⁰But we have dwelt in tents, and have obeyed, and done according to all that Jonadab our father commanded us.

¹¹But it came to pass, when Nebuchadnezzar king of Babylon came up into the land, that we said, Come, and let us go to Jerusalem for fear of the army of the Chaldeans, and for fear of the army of the Syrians: so we dwell at Jerusalem.

¹²Then came the word of the LORD unto Jeremiah, saying,

¹³Thus saith the LORD of hosts, the God of Israel; Go and tell the men of Judah and the inhabitants of Jerusalem, Will ye not receive instruction to hearken to my words? saith the LORD.

¹⁴The words of Jonadab the son of Rechab, that he commanded his sons not to drink wine, are performed; for unto this day they drink none, but obey their father's commandment: notwithstanding I have spoken unto you, rising early and speaking; but ye hearkened not unto me.

¹⁵I have sent also unto you all my servants the prophets, rising up early and sending them, saying, Return ye now every man from his evil way, and

amend your doings, and go not after other gods to serve them, and ye shall dwell in the land which I have given to you and to your fathers: but ye have not inclined your ear, nor hearkened unto me.

[16]Because the sons of Jonadab the son of Rechab have performed the commandment of their father, which he commanded them; but this people hath not hearkened unto me:

[17]Therefore thus saith the LORD God of hosts, the God of Israel; Behold, I will bring upon Judah and upon all the inhabitants of Jerusalem all the evil that I have pronounced against them: because I have spoken unto them, but they have not heard; and I have called unto them, but they have not answered.

[18]And Jeremiah said unto the house of the Rechabites, Thus saith the LORD of hosts, the God of Israel; Because ye have obeyed the commandment of Jonadab your father, and kept all his precepts, and done according unto all that he hath commanded you:

[19]Therefore thus saith the LORD of hosts, the God of Israel; Jonadab the son of Rechab shall not want a man to stand before me for ever.

Jeremiah was told to bring the Rechabites, a nomadic family, into the House of the Lord, and there serve them wine to drink. When Jeremiah attempted to do this, and brought them the wine, they said their father (ancestor) said we do not do that, and we will not.

Important points: the requirement not to drink wine can be argued as a biblical precept, but the building of houses and sowing of fields cannot. Therefore, this patriarch made extra biblical requirements for his family, **and they were obeyed for about 200 years!** If God was opposed to families setting standards not obvious in scripture, this was a wonderful opportunity for us to be told so. Instead, hear what the Lord's response was:

> *"Thus says the Lord of Hosts, the God of Israel; Because you have obeyed the commandment of Jonadab your father, and kept all his precepts and done according to all that he commanded you,*

*therefore ...Jonadab the son of Rechab shall not lack a man to stand before Me forever."*

There is a man, Bernando La Pallo, who was 113 years old at the time of an interview with him. He was asked the secret to his longevity. His response? "Obedience and moderation." I remember things my dad taught me when I was 8 years old." "He taught me how to live and how to eat, and God would take care of me. And so far, it has happened." Like the Rechabites, he had obeyed his father's instructions from over 100 years ago, and was walking in blessing!

In Rev. Larry Stockstill's fine book, "The Remnant," he points to a philosophy as a series of givens. It is a theory or attitude held by a person or organization that acts as a guiding principle for behavior. (Oxford American Dictionary). The givens are grounded on simplicity and godly sincerity. **Like the Rechabites, we need overarching principles to define and guide our decision-making.**

*"For our boasting is this: the testimony of our conscience that we conducted ourselves in the world in simplicity and godly sincerity, not with fleshly wisdom but by the grace of God and more abundantly toward you."*

- II Cor. 1:12, NKJV

## WHEN YOU CHANGE THE RULES

I remember twice changing the rules (or in one case the precedent) in our family.

In one case we had a policy against any martial arts shows being watched by our children. This was not the case due to philosophical or spiritual reasons. Our motives centered more around my kids thinking that landing on someone's neck would be fine since they do it on television with no harm done!

So, when our children were older, we called a family meeting. When everyone got together, the children wanted to know if Lonie was pregnant! (This was the usual reason in their mind for a family meeting). We explained we were changing our family rule, and why. This was the easy one.

The next time we changed a precedent established with our previous three children. Due to sports and other activities we decided to get a cell phone six months to one year before the other children got a phone. I assure you, England had less debate over entering World War Two than what we heard from the older three! Conference calls went to children in three cities, all weighing in on the significance of this change of policy. To this day it remains a topic that can set off heated debate.

The upside of this scandal is the seriousness our children took to the stability of the rules we kept in our home. This is the positive result of including children in the "why" behind our decisions, as well as the decisions themselves.

While the *rules* in the home occasionally changed, we were pretty careful about not changing the *standards* in the home. That is, what is permissible for our children to engage in, and at what point in their growth. I am referring to spiritual standards such as church attendance, secular music in the home, dating, and other areas of ethics that frankly defined who we are as a family.

**I totally respect my children's right and duty to make the standards for their homes in the future.** I am not responsible for their policies, only for my home. (Eze. 18)  Probably the greatest compliment any of our children ever gave us was noting "the standards in our house don't change."


"If you don't make your kids cry when they are little, they are going to make you cry when they are big."

-Wayne Austin

# CHAPTER FIVE:

## DOORS AND WINDOWS

"My neighbors loved the music so much when I turned it up, that they invited the police to listen."
- searchquotes.com

Doors and windows are designed to selectively choose what comes in and out of our house. Unlike walls, which always block entrance or exit, doors and windows give the option of allowing or barring people or things.

When I was an administrator of a Christian school, the high school supervisor and I noticed the number of times we would counsel a parent regarding their child's behavioral changes. Usually, there had been a decrease in interest in schoolwork or a change of friends. Sometimes the conversation centered on a personality switch: moodiness, depression, flaring of temper, or a fatalistic attitude toward life.   In this season of our ministry, we began discussing the idea that while the foundation and walls to the home might be secure, there was an open window or door where the enemy was coming in to attack the child.

Checking the Openings:

## MUSIC:

If the television has made inroads in the home in the last 50 years, music has greatly increased in influence and variety every bit as much.  Sound systems, ipods, MP3 players, all impact the children of today in profound ways.

Music is shown in Scripture to have a powerful influence in the soul's realm.  David was able to bring peace to Saul's torment through playing the harp (I Sam. 16).  We see the impact of music in II Ki. 3:15 when Elisha told the king of Israel to bring a musician.  When he played, the hand of the Lord came upon him, and he had direction from the Lord.

If you allow your children to listen to music that is secular, it is vital that you are aware of what is in the lyrics. While there are lyrics that are blasphemous and violent in nature, there are others whose message is one of defeat and fosters a sense of hopelessness and despair upon the listener. I had ministered to a young man who was depressed, and his mother was at a loss as to the source of his depression, not seeing anything in his life that would warrant such lethargy. Drugs were ruled out, and his academics were not a problem. His friends were not the greatest, but were not negative or depressed. By the grace of God, he brought his CD player to school one day, and it was taken from him. (They were not allowed at the Christian school.) The music consisted of talking, "Things will never get better, only worse. And your parents are telling you things get better, but they don't." No wonder he was depressed! Interestingly, this young man's friends listened to the same music and were less affected.

The type of lifestyle being lived by the performers is another area that should be addressed.  If the performer has the potential to reach "hero" status, it is vital that the conduct of the musician be one of merit.

Technology Quote: "By the way, if you get mad at your Mac laptop and wonder who designed this demonic device, notice the manufacturer's icon on top: an apple with a bite out of it."
— Peter Kreeft, *Jesus-Shock*

## COMPUTERS/IPADS/SMARTPHONES:

Years ago I had an unfortunate experience that probably occurs a thousand times each day. I was looking up something on the internet with my wife, transposed the website address, and up popped a pornographic site! I was shocked, and removed it, but this made me aware of how easy someone <u>not</u> looking for pornography could be exposed to it. Imagine the effortlessness with which one could find sexual material online if they are looking!

If any medium has made a new impact on culture, it is the computer. It has changed our vocabulary, conduct, business, and means of obtaining information. In addition, it has given unparalleled access to others, both desirable and undesirable.

Protecting children from negative influences on the internet has become a million dollar business. Statistics show that almost 90% of young men have viewed pornography on the internet, and about 25% of girls have looked at sexually explicit material, as well. (Carroll, Jason S., et al. "Generation XXX: Pornography Acceptance and Use Among Emerging Adults. Journal of Adolescent Research 23.1 (2008)

6-30. (Study examined population of emerging adults, aged 18-26))

There are filters for family computers, police specializing in catching online predators, and training for parents as to the hazards and benefits of online conversations. No filter, however, is sufficient to block all access to unsuitable material. A few cautions regarding the use of computers online by minors are in order.

1.  The computer should be in a public, frequently traveled area in the house. A child should never have an online computer in their bedroom.

2.  The computer should have a filter to prevent sexual websites. It is important to realize these are not 100% effective, but they help enormously. The filters not being always reliable is the reason for the minor to not have unguarded access.

3.  Your child should have his or her own log on for computer access, and you should have the password.  This enables you to see where on the internet they have gone, and when.

4.  If your child has a "Facebook" or other social media accounts, they should be set on "private," which prevents anyone from viewing the web page without your child's permission.  In addition, you should have your child's log-in name and password, and your child should know that you can view it at any time.  Finding vulgarity from a friend on your child's social media account should be reason to ban that friend, or close down the account. If your child believes they will lose their social media connections if you find

objectionable material, they will enforce your wishes.

5.  Chat rooms are a prime spot for sexual predators, and for people to misrepresent themselves to others.  I feel extreme caution should be used if a minor is allowed to access chat rooms. Picture downloads can be blocked on your child's account, and the child's need for having pictures sent can be done on your account.

6.  Parental uses of the Internet:
    a.  Screenit.com  Go to "No thanks" and then pull up any old or new movie for a complete breakdown of the film.
    b.  Pluggedin.com I believe is the James Dobson "Focus on the Family" site.

c. Other parental sites are available. Ask around or go online and find other resources.

Please, parents, I urge you not to think your son is "too good" to get caught in this. Simply put, you are delusional. This is a big deal. The potential impact of pornography on your child's future marriage is significant, but beyond the scope of our topic in this book.

**TELEVISION:**

Every time I go to my daughter and son-in-law's house, they have a new television. It's always bigger and clearer than the one before. They don't even watch much, as the ministry does not allow much time. I think the size of the television has replaced the size of a man' boat as a status symbol. "Oh, still using that 55" I see. I put in a 65" in the living room, and just decided, 'Why not go with a projection setup in the den?'"

As you know, one of the doors to your home is the television. How this is monitored is a key to your child growing up to be righteous, or "right-less!" The good news is there are means available to block programming that is a negative influence from coming into your home.  The bad news is there is usually a way around them if the child is defiant and determined to bypass the blocks. So what can be done about this door into our home?  Here are a few ideas that can be tried:

- The best way to keep control of the television is to keep it in a high traffic area where adults pass regularly.  A television in the child's bedroom guarantees there will be no oversight beyond the child's word that wrong messages are not being broadcast into your home.

- Buy or activate as many safeguard features as possible.
- In many cases the satellite company is able to block some stations from coming into your home. They will often refuse at first, saying it cannot be done, but often it can.
- Set times when the TV can be viewed.
- List the stations and shows that will not be allowed on in the house.

## RELATIONSHIPS:

God created us to be relational beings. While there are some who prefer isolation, the vast majority of us desire to have relationships. This can be a window we want opened or closed, obviously depending on the person involved!

The Scripture encourages us to have dealings with unbelievers.

In I Cor. 5:9-11, it says, "*I wrote to you in my epistle not keep company with sexually immoral people. Yet I certainly did not mean with the sexually immoral people of this world, or with the covetous, or extortioners...since then you would need to go out of the world...But now I have written to you not to keep company with anyone named a brother, who is sexually immoral, or covetous, or an idolater... or a drunkard...not even to eat with such a person.*"

The scripture is clear that our role as salt and light in the world will mean interaction with those who are not of the faith. However, I believe this applies primarily to adults. The influence a child's friend can have is enormous, and quite evident to anyone with children. Here are a few guidelines for parents to consider regarding relationships their children might have:

1. Know the child.  Inviting the child to come with the family will give you an opportunity to engage the child, and consider their potential impact.

2. Know the standards in the friend's home.  Are they different from your own?  They inevitably will be, but are they reasonably close to your own?  If not, are the child's parents willing to honor your standards when having your child over?

3. Do you know the parents?  Is there an opportunity for you to get to know them?  This will make you more comfortable in dealing with them.

## FINAL THOUGHTS ON DOORS AND WINDOWS:

Supervision of our children is one of the most important areas of child-rearing. We would be aghast if we knew of parents leaving their toddler by a pool unsupervised, yet many parents let their teen and pre-teen children go to movies, bowling alleys, and malls unsupervised every weekend. What guarantees are available if this becomes a meeting place for children you would not endorse? How would you know? To let our children go to public places in their early teens unsupervised is to throw open the doors of our children's lives to unseen forces. This can defeat the entire effort of guarding our children's best interests.

# CHAPTER SIX:

THE ROOF

"Parental Authority"

# I. Providing Spiritual Authority for our Children

(Much of this material I learned from John Bevere's excellent book, "Under Cover", and Watchman Nee's classic, "Spiritual Authority".)

As the person God has delegated to train your children in godliness, it is vital that we fulfill our roles and our children stay under our authority, for that is where God's blessing resides. It is interesting that scripture states, *"Cursed is the man who dishonors his father or mother."* Note it is a "man" who must honor his parents, not just children. Of course, that does not mean grown children must obey their parents, but a culture of honor in the family should never end!

We need our children to be both obedient, which is their actions, and submissive, which is in attitude. (I Chr. 28:9, Heb. 13:17)
The three times it is permissive for children to question (or appeal) your decision are:

1. If the decision directly contradicts scripture (Ex. 1:17ff, Ac. 4:18-20, Dan. 6:10)
2. There is information that was not available when you made the original decision (I Sam. 25)
3. Role of intercessor on behalf of another (Ex. 32:11-14)

FATHERS

Fathers, you are the key to your family serving God or not. It is certainly possible for children to grow up and serve the Lord with a father who is not a believer, but it is much harder. **Both parents must remember that they are not**

**called to be their child's friend, but their parent.** If the parenting is done well, the grown children will often turn out to be our best friends, and vice versa. But in friendships, the one with the strongest personality becomes the leader, and your child is not old enough or wise enough to fill that role.

Being friendly with your children is fine, but they must know there is a line you are able to step across and again assert authority.

I once had a student who I was correcting. The child was new to the school, and thought I was joking. The other students began warning the child he was going too far. Their counsel was not heeded, and I wound up having to suspend the student from all activities.

When the child realized I was quite serious, he apologized profusely and begged for another chance. One of my favorite verses in the New Testament is Titus 2:11-12, which explains that it is the "*grace of God that brings salvation...it teaches us to say "No" to ungodliness...and to live self-*

*controlled, upright and godly lives in this present age*." I reinstated the student, and we became very close for the remainder of their time in our school.

## Increasing our faith

An aspect of obedience not familiar to most Christians is that it increases our faith. Look at Lk. 17:1-6. The disciples asked the Lord to "increase their faith." Most people think Jesus' answer is that they only need a small amount of faith, like a mustard seed. But the paragraph and the Lord's thought does not end there. He continues with a conjunction and points to a story where the servant does his job, obeying his master, and this ends the teaching.

A second example, and one easier to understand, occurs when the centurion comes with a prayer request in Matt. 8:8-9. Jesus sees the revelation this Gentile has and declares He has not seen this kind of faith in all of Israel!

## Children being Deceived

Deception can be found all the way back to early Genesis, where Satan tricked Eve. (Gen. 3-6, II Cor. 11:3) Children can be deceived from obeying a couple of ways. **One is rationalizing**.

If our child desires to do some activity you have forbidden, and he or she does it anyway, and nothing bad happens, he or she will decide they were right, and you were wrong. "I knew it would be okay if I went to the concert. And I'm sorry I had to lie about where I'd be, but nothing bad happened, just like I said." This short-term success appears to validate the rebellion.

The second way children are deceived is when **they hear God's word, and do not do it**. (Ja. 1:22)

How do we protect our children from deception? Three ways are given:

    1. Developing a Fear of the Lord (Ps. 25:14)
       My wife was upset one day because she would see our children obey me quicker

than her. She said, "It's because they are scared of you." I guess she meant that was a bad thing. Anyway, at supper that night I asked the kids, "Are you afraid of your daddy?" They replied, "No." I said, "What if you have done something wrong?" They said, "Then, yeah, we are afraid." I informed my wife, Lonie, things were pretty much just the way I wanted them!

2. Humility (Is. 66:2) For us to develop humility (not humiliation) in our children is so valuable! But to accomplish this we have to be examples, and that is so hard for some of us!

3. Revelation Knowledge (I Jn. 2:26-27) When there is a proper fear of the Lord and humility, we can expect to see the Lord reveal Himself to our children in a great way! This protects them as the Lord will

reveal to them where they are going astray.

We must see rebellion as the Lord sees it. (I Sam. 15:22-23) The Lord calls it "witchcraft" and "idolatry." Sounds pretty serious! Scripture goes on to teach that we place ourselves under a curse through disobedience. (Gal. 3:1)

Remember that we are always preparing our children to be leaders- whether of churches, businesses or homes. God's goal in our lives and theirs is brokenness (I Pet. 2:13-21)

# II. WHEN KIDS FAIL (or Making Big Deals Out of Little Deals and Little Deals out of Big Deals)

This may be the most important chapter in this book. Certainly, if you encounter a situation like the one expressed here, I truly believe it will change how you approach discipline for the better.

I have had to speak with parents on several occasions regarding knowledge their son or daughter was involved either in secret relationships that were harmful, or activities that would lead to destruction. The responses from some parents were illustrative of what *not* to do.

- One parent (who I knew well) chewed me out for accusing her child. All I had said was her daughter was leaving school with students I knew were living destructive lifestyles.

- Another's child was getting sexually active, and spending time as a high school sophomore in a dangerous area on the university campus at night in the next town. They thanked me. Spent the evening in an enjoyable manner with their daughter, then informed me all was well. This turned out not to be the case.

- A third parent listened, and did nothing outward about the news. (I am sure all of these parents prayed.)

The different responses of attacking the bearer of news, the glossing over the decisions their child was making, and the simple ignoring of the information- none of these bore good fruit. The problem is none of us are sure what to do when our kids fail to live by the guidelines we have instilled in them.

We all have times when we are proud of our children: graduation, handling a situation well, hitting the game-winning run, being a soloist, or placing superior in a music event.

Other times we feel disappointment at our children's decisions: not studying for an exam as much as they should, or getting interested in a guy or girl we don't feel good about, or not responding to a situation in the manner we taught them.

But then there are other times, thankfully not many, when our children fail completely in the "big test." This is when the police show up to say that our child has been arrested. Or that our child is pregnant or got someone pregnant. Perhaps we discover drugs in our child's bag in the closet, maybe enough to indicate it is for sale, not just their personal use. **It is at these times that we wonder if everything we have done has been a waste of time**.

## Kim's Story

Kim was a quality honors student who had never given her mom any major problems. Minor infractions were occasional (a little late for curfew, not finishing household chores, etc.) but never got a single demerit at school. Kim's mom, Janet, got the surprise of her life one day when the school called to notify her that Kim had gotten drunk at a weekend party.

Kim was brought to the principal of the Christian school she attended, and was asked to tell her story. Because she had a good relationship with the administrator, she opened up.

As the rest of the details came out, it was apparent Kim had been drinking for over a year, going to harder alcohol as she progressed in her partying. The conversation was sad, but had its humorous moments:

Me: "So how many of you were there and what were you drinking?

Kim: "There were five of us. I was drinking tequila."

Me: "I bet you've been drinking six months."

Kim: "How could you know that? Did God show you?"

Me: "No, you've been dating an unbeliever for six months. It made sense. Also, I didn't grow up in church. And I never

knew anyone who started with tequila."

The principal and parents got together, and decided to work together on Kim's punishment. Kim was obviously repentant, and humiliated as a result of her actions being uncovered. She was forthright about the rest of her activities, and was open to whatever retribution was meted out.

It seems counter-intuitive, but the key here is when a child does something wrong, we should correct it in a big way. But when the child of a Christian home really blows it (pregnant, substance abuse, or whatever), they do not need to be lashed. Like the prodigal son, he or she knows no mercy is available, no extra chances. And this is when you as the parent get to become their hero.

**Dads, it will mean so much more if you are the leader on this**. In fact, you should be the leader when it comes to discipline, correction, and forgiveness with any child above a toddler.

Coming alongside our child, loving him or her, offering our sympathy for the situation, and our encouragement- this will shock the child, the gratitude will flow, and you might see the tragedy of the situation turn into a new dimension of intimacy with your child.

**By the way, Kim is now married and last I heard was working in full time ministry!**

Paul understood this feeling, when he said in Gal. 1:6, "*I marvel that you are turning away so soon from Him who called you in the grace of Christ, to a different gospel*" and then later in the epistle states, "*I am afraid for you, lest I have labored for you in vain.*" But perhaps the greatest example of the gut-twisting, hope, and eventual success that comes with watching our failure is found in the familiar story of the Prodigal Son, in Lk. 15: 11-32.

Points of Interest in the story of the Prodigal Son:

1. **The son turned his back on everything the father stood for**: we know the dad disapproved of his younger son's lifestyle by the reaction of the older son: v.29-30 *"All these years I've worked hard for you and never refused to do a single thing you told me to….Yet this son of yours comes back after squandering your money on prostitutes"* So we see the father was a moral man, who had raised his sons to be moral.

2. **He left his father no hope of things changing.**

   -The son left physically, leaving no information as to his plans or future address.

   - He left emotionally when he said give me my share. He was cutting himself off from his father and brother.

   - He tried to leave spiritually, but the father was a man of hope.

This is the turning point of hope.  What the son knew!

3. **The son knew his father's integrity.**   He knew that his father was always fair to his workers.

4. **The son knew his father's mercy.**  He knew he would be received if he returned.

5.  **The son discovered his father's love.** There was no way to know the depth of his father's love until he needed it the most.

I have found the focus of dealing with children falling is counterintuitive: when a child disappoints in a minor way, make a big deal out of it. This enforces the boundaries and shows we are not bending what is expected. When the child's actions cause a massive collapse of everything, we show mercy. Why? Because the child already knows they have failed. They are standing ashamed, awaiting the harsh judgment they realize they deserve. The story of Rehoboam seems pertinent here:

Rehoboam went to Shechem, where all Israel had gathered to make him king. ² When Jeroboam son of Nebat heard of this, he returned from Egypt,[a] for he had fled to Egypt to escape from King Solomon. ³ The leaders of Israel summoned him, and Jeroboam and the whole assembly of Israel went to speak with Rehoboam. ⁴ "Your father was a hard master," they said. "Lighten the harsh labor demands and heavy taxes that your father imposed on us. Then we will be your loyal subjects."

Rehoboam replied, "Give me three days to think this over. Then come back for my answer." So the people went away.

Then King Rehoboam discussed the matter with the older men who had counseled his father, Solomon. "What is your advice?" he asked. "How should I answer these people?"

*The older counselors replied, "If you are willing to be a servant to these people today and give them a favorable answer, they will always be your loyal subjects."* I Kings 12:1-7

A couple of other points regarding when kids fail:

- **There should never be doubt about your disapproval of their sin, but there should always be communication and love**. In Jn. 4, Jesus talks with a Samaritan woman, and confronts her sin. V. 17 *"You have five husbands, and the one whom you now have is not your husband…"* This does not cause her to feel condemned and leave, rather she continues talking with the Lord and realizes He is the Messiah.
- **If we cut off because of their lifestyle or mistakes, we decrease our chance to be the "father of the prodigal."** We can be

fearful that our friendship will be perceived as approval. Believe me; our children know what we believe! But the closeness of our relationship will make it easier when he "comes to himself." Lk. 15:17 *"But when he finally came to his senses..."* (NLT)

- **Spend more time thinking on what the Lord has promised than on what you are seeing.**

    -Noah built an ark when there was no rain

    -Gideon was called a "mighty man of valor" when                      he was hiding in a winepress.

    -The examples are many. Just remember the

    words of Martin Luther. He said, "Pray, let God worry."

The prodigal did come home, to a grand reunion, and they did live happily ever after. **If you are still like the father, "looking with compassion," there is hope. Not in our child, but in the God who cares.**

The absence of a religious upbringing unfailingly manifests itself in a person's character - a sort of fissure can be perceived in his spiritual makeup. A child is extraordinarily receptive to religious impressions. He is instinctively drawn toward everything that opens up the beauty and meaning of life. Take this away from him and his soul will become dulled and he will feel lonely in an unfriendly and cruel world.

- Bishop Alexander (Mileant)

# CHAPTER SEVEN:

# FURNISHINGS

"Few things build a person up like affirmation. According to Webster's New World Dictionary, Third College Edition (Simon and Schuster, 1991), the word "affirm" comes from *ad firmare*, which means "to make firm." **So when you affirm people, you make firm within them the things you see about them**. Do that often enough, and the belief that solidifies within them will become stronger than the doubts they have about themselves."

— John C. Maxwell

**Things you never say to your child:**

- **"I thought you got saved."** When our child gets back from church camp, retreat, or a service, and we hear they got saved, we are immediately filled with great joy.  But, like us, they are not perfect!  The worst thing we can say to our child after their committing their lives to the Lord, and letting us down later that week, is, I thought you got saved." It is important to remember there are only two markers on our journey in Christ: Where did I start? And the Image of Christ. It takes time for progress to develop from one to the other. As time goes by, we should be able to look back and see that we are godlier now than we were a year ago. Its all about the direction we are headed. Have you ever wondered why an unsaved person can be more godly than someone who is born again? Let's look at two points on a line:

............1.......................2..........+++

Lets say number 1 represents the morality of a new believer. He really doesn't know much, because he was not raised with Christian principles. Now, let's say the number 2 represents a girl who was raised in a moral home, and incorporated Christian principles in her life, though she never got saved. To the observer, she is more "Christian" than the boy, yet he is going to heaven, and she will not until she accepts Jesus as her savior. Obviously, there should come a time when the believer would exhibit more Christ-like behavior than she does, but it is not an instant change! Charging your child with this accusation in effect calls your child a hypocrite, a surefire way to cause them to fall away and not make future attempts to serve the Lord. No son or daughter wants to be labeled as a hypocrite!

- **Why can't you be like your brother, sister, etc."** God created each of our children uniquely, and He has plans that are specific to each. They are not more like their sibling because they are not their sibling! Though they were not siblings, two men in the Bible had a relationship with the apostle Paul. Mark abandoned Paul and Barnabas on their first missions trip- not an auspicious beginning to his ministry! Demas was faithful, traveling with Paul on his evangelistic team from city to city. How surprising toward the end of Paul's life that he writes, "*Be diligent to come to me quickly; for Demas has forsaken me, having loved this present world, and has departed...Only Luke is with me. Get Mark and bring him with you, for he is useful to me for ministry.*" Many times the willful child is the one who will get more done for the Lord than the compliant child. The Spirit has a way of taking the strong willed child and bringing that will under control, and using it to advance the Kingdom of God!

- **Attacking Christian things they like because it is not our "style."**

    I am old enough to know that the Christian music of the 70s was not well received by the good men and women of the church! The instruments, rhythms and lyrics were contemporary, and did not fit the hymns or camp meeting tunes. But coming out of a rock background, I loved it. Now I am at the other end, cringing at some of the forms of Christian music out today. A study of General Booth's approach to outreach, along with John Wesley, would be helpful to anyone wrestling with this. I have seen Christian parents with all the best intentions in the world forbid their children to listen to current Christian music. They would do well to rejoice their children desire to listen to Christian music. The same goes for any other cultural phenomenon that does not directly contradict Christian values. One line that could help is if the dress or actions are to draw attention to the Christian child. That is not biblical, and should be approached that way.

- **"You are embarrassing me."**
  Regardless of what is meant by the speaker, the message is not concern for the child who is acting wrong, but for the reputation of the parent. This gets into "I love you if...", or conditional love.

Part of the responsibility of the parent is to get your child excited about God. We will look at this next. (Hint: you cannot get your child excited about God! Only He can! So, what's your role?)

## The Three Chairs

Bruce Wilkinson, maybe best known for his incredible little book, <u>The Prayer of Jabez</u>, had an amazing revelation of how children grow up in Christian homes, and what impact it makes on them. In his series, "The Three Chairs," Wilkinson explained using subsequent generations, that each generation must have their own first-hand encounter with the Lord. Wilkinson points to Ju. 2:7-10, for his model:

> "So the people served the Lord all the days of Joshua, and all the days of the elders who outlived Joshua, who had seen all the great works of the Lord which he had done for

*Israel. Now Joshua the son of Nun, the servant of the Lord, died when he was one hundred and ten years old. And they buried him within the border of his inheritance at Timnath Heres, in the mountains of Ephraim, on the north side of Mount Gaash. When all that generation had been gathered to their fathers, another generation arose after them who did not know the Lord nor the wok which He had done for Israel."* (KJV)

The keys to understanding are symbolized by three chairs. In this passage, Joshua would represent the first chair- those who did the works of God.

The second chair would be the elders who outlived Joshua, who had seen the works of God.

The third chair is the generation which did not know the Lord nor the work which He had done for Israel.

Those in the first chair are the ones who had an incredible encounter with the Lord. These are first generation Christians, or Christians who have experienced the works of the Lord in their personal lives. Their testimony is fresh- God is continuing to show Himself in the fruit of their living. They live to please God, not themselves. They are committed to putting the Lord first, and serving their fellow man as the result of their relationship with Jesus. They are devoted, and their decisions are based on Scripture.

Rich Wilkinson explains that **the people who occupy the second chair are often the children of those in the first chair.** They are the elders who had seen and heard the works of God. They grew up hearing and seeing God work in their parents' lives. They grew up hearing their parents asking the Lord for His direction and purpose in their lives. But they have not had a personal experience, and thus their lives are ones of compromise. Christianity is for Sundays, and their God-relationship is based on responsibility, not heart-felt devotion. Their standards rise and fall based on other Christians, rather than the Scriptures. They have a divided heart. They are more concerned with possessions than people. They put their own desires ahead of the Lord.

Those sitting in the third chair have not had a personal experience with the Lord Jesus Christ. They grew up in a home of "me first" Christians, attending church "because it's the right thing to do," and putting things ahead of people. When they ask for stories of God moving in the family, their stories revolve around the grandparents, those who lived in the first chair. They did not grow up hearing the question, "What does God want?" Christianity was a Sunday religion, not a daily relationship. Is it any wonder that as they grow up they have no interest in the things of God?

The obvious question is, "How do I insure that my children live in the first chair, and not the other two?"

Is there anything more important to those who know the Lord than seeing their children grow up to integrate in their personal lives the spiritual calling and priorities they have been raised to honor? Why do some children raised in Christian homes continue in the Way throughout their lives, while others fall away and return when they are older? Still others leave when they go to college or get out of the house and never return. Many tears have fallen and sleepless nights have taken place over our seeming failure to lead our children to inculcate the values and hunger for Jesus Christ we have attempted to instill in their hearts. Were we so terrible in our witness that they want no part of Christ? Do they not understand the wonderful works of God with which He has blessed us, both individually and as a family?

A more specific question that arises is why do we lose a larger percentage of boys than girls? Especially boys with leadership qualities? Honestly, we wonder who is to blame. Is it the pastor? The youth pastor? Our spouse? Could it actually be me?

**What is not going to help is cross-examining our offspring, going to ludicrous lengths to encourage, threaten, bribe, or nag them into the Kingdom**. I am not the Holy Spirit- shoot, some days I am flowing more in the flesh than the Spirit- and the chances of me using fleshly means to see godly ends does not make sense. Does any of the following sound familiar?

- Honey, don't you want to raise your hands during worship, like you used to do?
- Why don't you sing instead of just standing there?
- I noticed two of your friends went to the altar the other day. Don't you feel like you should, too?
- I saw the youth pastor cutting up with Sally and Joanie. Don't you want to go hang with him?

**What is wrong with you?** You better be careful because I'm not sure Jesus is real pleased with you. I'm sure you can come up with your own. With all my heart I sympathize, but it is my experience none of this does any good. "Can't I say anything?" Yes, but there is a time and it is providential.

## Dealing with Christian families with different values

"*There is nothing wrong with Halloween! That's one of my favorite memories as a child!*" "*I think bringing a Christmas tree in one's home is idolatry! The Bible says so, somewhere I think. We shouldn't be worshiping trees.*" *Is it okay for my child to be Karate? Is it really part of an eastern religion? Just stay away from Disney! I heard someone say Mickey Mouse is the Antichrist.*" "*We don't believe in going to doctors. Those with faith don't need them.*"

I have heard all of these in my Christian walk, (yeah, even the one about Mickey Mouse), and this brings into clear view **an aspect of raising Godly kids that can alternate between encouragement and frustration- interaction with other Christian families**.

When one finds a family with similar values (what is permissible to watch, do, say, etc.) it is so pleasant to connect with them. The children see the values with which they are being raised supported by another set of parents, whose children are inculcated with similar mores. Conversely, when we spend time with Christian families who are far more permissive, or have a different perspective on living holy, we are perplexed. How do we answer our children's legitimate questions? "Mom, don't they love Jesus?" "Why do they allow their son to watch sinful shows on TV?" I've said it before, but it bears repeating. One can get so upset over the repeated questions that the thought comes to mind, "*Because Jimmy's family is going to hell, dear, and we do not want you to go there.*" Obviously this is not going to be said, but you might have wanted to! (Okay, maybe that's just me thinking that.)

In summary, while we cannot force our children to be on fire for God, we can increase the odds dramatically.

"*Let parents bequeath to their children not riches, but the spirit of reverence.*" - Plato

"*If your kids are giving you a headache, follow the directions on the aspirin bottle, especially the part that says, 'keep away from children.'*"
- Susan Savanna

# Section II

## CHAPTER EIGHT:

## HOW TO GET YOUR CHILD SAVED

### (hint: You can't!)

We all want our children to be on fire for the Lord. We want them to fall in love with Jesus, to experience the radical transformation we had when we came to Him.

As I pointed out in the previous chapter citing Bruce Wilkinson, we want our children in the "first chair." **The fact remains we cannot replace the Holy Spirit's work in the human heart!**

What we *can* do is lay the groundwork for our children to be prepared when the Lord sends the fire, which we believe He will- after all, He loves our children more than we do!

The story of the prophet, Elijah, on Mt. Carmel gives a great illustration of what our role is in the spiritual transformation of our children:

*Then Elijah said to all the people, "Come near to me." So all the people came near to him. And he repaired the altar of the LORD that was broken down. 31 And Elijah took twelve stones, according to the number of the tribes of the sons of Jacob, to whom the word of the LORD had come, saying, "Israel shall be your name."[b] 32 Then with the stones he built an altar in the name of the LORD; and he made a trench around the altar large enough to hold two seahs of seed. 33 And he put the wood in order, cut the bull in pieces, and laid it on the wood, and said, "Fill four waterpots with water, and pour it on the burnt sacrifice and on the wood." 34 Then he said, "Do it a second time," and they did it a second time; and he said, "Do it a third time," and they did it a third time. 35 So the water ran all around the altar; and he also filled the trench with water.*

³⁶ And it came to pass, at the time of the offering of the evening sacrifice, that Elijah the prophet came near and said, "LORD God of Abraham, Isaac, and Israel, let it be known this day that You are God in Israel and I am Your servant, and that I have done all these things at Your word. ³⁷ Hear me, O LORD, hear me, that this people may know that You are the LORD God, and that You have turned their hearts back to You again."

³⁸ Then the fire of the LORD fell and consumed the burnt sacrifice, and the wood and the stones and the dust, and it licked up the water that was in the trench. ³⁹ Now when all the people saw it, they fell on their faces; and they said, "The LORD, He is God! The LORD, He is God!"

⁴⁰ And Elijah said to them, "Seize the prophets of Baal! Do not let one of them escape!" So they seized them; and Elijah brought them down to the Brook Kishon and executed them there.    I Kings 18:30ff

(Presentation 8 on Powerpoint)

142

So what was Elijah's role in bringing the fire to the altar?

- **He had great trust in the Lord**. He challenged the Jewish people; he threw down the gauntlet to the idolatrous priests, and even poured water on the altar.
- **Elijah repaired the altar**. This means he rededicated his own efforts to worship. He was reminding the people of when this altar was used to honor Jehovah. This prophet's labor was a visual of the need for the children of the Promise to worship the true God.

- **He prepared the sacrifice**. Elijah was doing the dirty, necessary effort to have a pleasing offering unto the Lord.

**But only God could send the fire**! This is the crucial aspect of raising children to be alive in Christ. Your children have a free will. Some Christian family experts have almost guaranteed children who love and serve Jesus Christ if you follow the "formula." This is bad theology. There is no biblical precedent of godly people having automatically devoted children.

**Well, that isn't encouraging**! The encouragement is coming, hang in there. Our role as parents and spiritual leaders of our offspring involves doing what Elijah did on Mt. Carmel.

1. <u>We trust the Lord</u>. As soon as we believe that we control whether our children have the fire of God we are trying to "earn" godly children. **Any aspect of Christianity that stresses my efforts over God's grace is wrong!** Elijah trusted the Lord's love for His people-do we? This is fundamental to our children serving God. If I am responsible for their commitment to the Lord then I am going

to put personal pressure and offer conditional love (if you don't embarrass me at church functions, if you are a student youth leader, etc., then I am proud of you). If we think our children do not see through this we are sadly mistaken. Obviously when our children are small, their imitations of us worshipping are wonderful and inspiring. But when they get older, we must be careful not to take God's place. When one of my children was a new teenager, she was lifting her hands and worshipping. A sweet lady in the church remarked at how much she enjoyed seeing my girl seeking God, and my daughter stopped for a couple of years. She was very self-conscious that others were watching her in church. We were heart-broken, of course, but tried not to push the issue hard. (We did try to get her to ignore what others did, but to no avail. I realized we had to let this go.)

2. <u>We have to repair (or maintain) the altar</u>.

I have talked about family devotions in another chapter, but I want to say again there is a lot of importance in having what used to be called a family altar. It is great that church is a place our children recognize as a place God should be honored. It is every bit as important our home is also regarded as such. This may involve repair- we might not have a history of having a Bible time in our house. We might have a weekly conversation of whether we are going to church this weekend. I urge you not to have that dialogue. At times we discussed which service we were attending, but going to church was non-negotiable.

3. <u>We have to prepare the sacrifice.</u> **To me, this means I have set up everything to prepare my child to catch fire**. This involves:

    a. Speaking well of the church and its leaders.

    As adults, we can see strengths and weaknesses in people's lives. We know pastors and other leaders at church are human, and make mistakes (You do know that, don't you?). Teens see spiritual matters in black and white. They do not tolerate sin, errors in judgment, or human character flaws in someone who is supposed to represent the Lord.

b. Putting my child in every situation possible for the Holy Spirit to speak to my child's heart.

My wife and I placed high priority in our children going on missions trips, even as small children. They were in lower elementary when they celebrated Christmas in mountain villages in southern Mexico. These remote villages did not even speak Spanish, only Mayan dialects! The videos we made have reminded our children of these trips.

We have encouraged our children to go to every Kid's Camp, Youth Camp, retreat, special service, and any other setting we thought might be a connect point for our children to meet the Lord Jesus Christ.

c. Making church a priority

I cringe when I see good Christian parents skipping church on a regular basis for sporting events and other activities. The argument goes like this: "My child is more important than church. Church doesn't equal God." Quite true. **The problem is your child *does* equate church with God**, and you just told them softball, soccer, or whatever, is more important than the Lord. We had two children play travel ball, so we faced this dilemma. It is such a testimony to the other players. They will ask, "Why can't you miss church?" What an opportunity to speak to the vital role Christianity places in our family!

# CHAPTER NINE:

# CURFEWS, GROUNDING, AND OTHER VIOLATIONS OF THE EIGHTH AMENDMENT *

## (* that's the one about cruel and unusual punishment)

*"YOU'RE MAKING IT DIFFICULT FOR ME TO BE THE PARENT I WANT TO BE."*

Curfews, Grounding, and Punishment in General

If only Adam and Eve had not messed up! But do not be too hard on them; if you or I were there we would have blown it, too. Fallen nature requires discipline, which at times requires punishment and limits on personal freedom.

**Curfews**

I assume you will see the need of curfews for your child. There are a few children who are very introverted, and may not be the "going out" type. I have one of those. Only one. The rest needed some set of guidelines. A few thoughts on what your rules for curfews should include:

- What you set for the first one will set a precedent for subsequent children. And boy, are you going to hear about it if you allow number three more leeway than you did one and two! It is important not let your child "play" you by saying that their friends have no curfew, or it is ridiculous. In some cases it may be true, but here is the key: **your decisions are not based on other parents, but on what the Scripture and the Holy Spirit's leading**.

- You will need to decide the punishment before they show up late.

- You need some way to know if they broke curfew. Some use an alarm clock in the parent's room. If it goes off, so do you.
- Knowing where your child is can affect special permission to change the curfew (down the street at a godly friend's house, for example). If you ever doubt your child is where they claim, tell them to take a picture of the parent's car, or the parent, or some other creative idea, and tell them to send it to your phone right away. (Isn't technology great!)
- It's tempting to alter curfews for sons as opposed to daughters. I would recommend against it.

## Grounding

Each child has a personality that lends itself to a particular correction being successful. I have a son who loved reading. Telling him to go to his room was fine- he wanted to be there anyway, so he could read in peace. My other son wanted to play so badly he would beg for a spanking so he could rejoin his friends outside. When grounding is used, the parent must have a few aspects of the punishment clear in their mind before implementing the sentence.

1. The duration must make sense, and be enforceable. If you tell your child they cannot leave their room after school for a week, and there is ball practice, a birthday party in the family, and/or a church event, does the   grounding influence these? If there is an event almost each day, is the child really grounded at all? This must be thought through.

2. The duration must be clear. I warned one of my kids that if they were not nicer to their sibling when people slept over, my older child would be grounded for the whole summer. This wound up having to be employed. The grounding was simple: no sleep overs, and no sleeping at anyone else's house. We

made an exception in the middle of the summer for their birthday, but that was it. We never had a problem with this again.

I remember an episode of Happy Days, when Richie, the son, got in trouble. He tells one of his friends, "I'm grounded for life! Can they do that?"

3. The "mercy" parent cannot be allowed to give in. If so, the two of you will have the reputation with your children that grounding is a joke, and never lasts as long as you say. This means your word is not good. Ps. 15 says the righteous man "keeps his oath even when it hurts." Paradoxically, you <u>owe</u> it to your child to ground them as long as you say, so be careful what you say! Make sure both of you are in agreement. This means we do not issue edicts of grounding spontaneously.

4. One of the toughest tricks with grounding is extra-curricular activities involving other members of the team or troupe. We do not wish to hurt others

for our child's errors. I would recommend caution in this area.

5. Another difficult area is midweek church- Am I going to forbid going to youth group because it is an opportunity for social interaction? Decide on this and spell it out up front for your child. Much better to plan before than being caught off guard.

Working with the School in Discipline

I have to confess this is an important topic to me. I have had the privilege to teach in public and private schools, both elementary and secondary. For the about 20 years I have worked in administration. The difference in the results achieved when the parent is a willing partner with the school is dramatic.

The first key to success in helping our child learn to flow in the school atmosphere is to support the those in leadership. Many times I have been able to help a family, and see their child succeed, because of the parents' unflinching support of our leadership. This sounds old fashioned, but we knew if we had to correct the student, that child was going to get corrected again at home. In some cases we could not have kept the child in the school, as his behavior would not have permitted it.

When the parents are distrustful, or accuse the leadership of being unfair, or arbitrary in our discipline, usually the result was the child being removed from the school (by administration or by the parents). This was followed by the child transferring to another school. Surprisingly (not really), the parents were upset with the next school's discipline. And so on it would go.

This cannot be made any more clearly- if you do not respect the teacher, or the administration, you should remove your child from the setting. (The same goes for the pastor in the pulpit; if you cannot honor the man in the pulpit, get out of the pew. But I digress...)

Assuming the teacher is genuinely interested in your child's success, you should be willing to follow their suggestions. In some cases the teacher has interacted with thousands of children- certainly hundreds. Most students fall into some category in the teacher's experience, and he or she has seen what worked and what did not.

Well, what is the parent to do when there are legitimate questions regarding the teacher's actions, or the teacher's actions violated the school or classroom policies? In this situation, the parent should arrange for a meeting with the teacher to bring this to their attention. If this should fail to solve the issue, then the next person in the chain of command should be contacted. This is consistent with the teachings of Matt. 18, and is the Christian method of resolving disputes.

When the need arises to speak to the child's authority, the best way to handle this is to do so without the knowledge of the child. If the child thinks he can go to you and you will go to battle on their behalf, the student will bring you into battle quite often. In fact, you may never take off your armor! I will address this in more detail in a later section.

One of my children had a beef with a different teacher every year. Only once did I find his superior to be in serious error. This was corrected, and we were able to move forward.

Most of the times I have had to remove a child from our school, it was because of the difficulty in working with the parents. Rarely have I had parents who supported our staff and policies but were unable to reach the child.


Working with Coaches and Ancillary Authorities in Your Child's Life

I was coaching a softball team, and had a new student with an aggressive, teasing attitude. I was not happy with the effort put forth in practice that day, and the new player began clowning around as I was correcting the players. I told the girl to stop, but she continued making inappropriate comments. I sternly warned her (as coaches can do), but she did not heed the tone. The other players began warning her, but she did not take the hint. Finally, I said she needed to put her uniform on my desk first thing tomorrow morning, and I walked off. She was shocked, and the next morning I found the uniform clean and folded, with a note apologizing for her behavior and begging to be reinstated. I met with the young lady, let her return to the team, and we had a great relationship to this day. Fortunately, her parents allowed the scenario to play out without interfere Had they called and ordered me to put her back on the team, I would have been unable to reinstate her. To do so would have been conceding control of the team.

Another incident (there are so many) was with a student on my basketball team. It was our first year and we were not very good. Our first game was not going well, and I played everyone on the bench. All the students got in the game but one girl who did not get on the court the entire game, which was a blowout. The parents couldn't wait for the buzzer to come chew me out for not playing their girl. "What harm could it have done to let our girl in for a few minutes? We came to the game to see her play and you would not let her on the court." Boy, they were hot. I waited until their diatribe concluded, then explained I had tried to put her in but she had refused. She was afraid. Things done (or not done) by those in authority can have a reason and purpose of which we were not aware.

Coaches are underpaid, overworked, and get too much credit for wins and too much blame for losses. The coach that is into coaching for his or her own glory is easy to discern, and unless the child is going to play at the next level should not play for that leader.

Too often, parents perspective of their son or daughter's ability is skewed. There is simply no objectivity in most parents evaluating their offspring's athletic prowess. I once had a parent come tell me to force the baseball coach to play his son in the infield. Our coach had been an assistant coach at a nationally acclaimed program. He knew more about baseball than I ever will. I refused to talk to the coach, and told the parent that was his concern, not mine. He did talk to the coach, and the coach surprised me by playing the child in the next game. It was a non-district game. The dad stood proud as a peacock with the other fathers, watching his child paly in the infield. Do I need to relate what happened? The young man made two errors in the last inning and cost the team the game. While I never would have allowed the player to be placed there, it did serve the purpose. The dad never complained again.

# CHAPTER TEN:

# BLENDED FAMILIES

"Of these expectations, I find the most common mistake that new step-parents make is in expecting these "new" kids to automatically love them. For the most part, it just doesn't happen that way. The greatest gift you can give to your new blended family is to give the children plenty of time – even a year or two – to figure out that you're safe, worthwhile, and then, maybe even likeable. But of course, that will only happen if it's true.
http://www.selfgrowth.com/articles/The_Blended_Family_Hopes_Fears_and_Tasks.html

Estimates are that 40% of all married couples in the United States with children are blended or stepfamilies. There are many resources on blended families, but to ignore this percentage of households in a parenting book seems grossly negligent, so I will attempt to emphasize a few points I have drawn in counseling and educating over several decades.

Becoming a parent in a blended family is obviously easier if the children are young, and if the biological parent of the same gender is no longer interacting in the child's life. But what if the children are older, and the natural parent you are replacing in the home is still around?

1. Children are not necessarily going to accept the love of the new adult.

Often the biological parent assumes their offspring are ready to accept a new "mom" or "dad." Actually the opposite is probably closer to reality. How should the stepfather or stepmother handle the new role? With regard to affection, the new parent must let the child come at their comfort level, not that of the adult. The interactions need to be positive as much as possible. The stages may be going from casual friend, to true friendship, to advisor, to parent. One cannot order someone to love another- a child cannot control that emotion. If great care is exercised there can come a point where the stepparent has a vital role in the child's life. Being kind to the child will help. Children who have gone through the pain of a divorce are not going to "fall in love" with the family or individual being blended into their lives. The process will be more like tending a hard-to-grow, delicate flower. There will be times of tending, fertilizing and provision to see success in the relationship. One thing that all stepparents can do is praise and encourage each of the children. It is amazing how much good this does. If nothing comes to mind, a text saying that you love them and are proud of them will do wonders.

2. Children are not necessarily going to accept the authority of the new adult.

   a. New Stepmoms

      I once taught a young man whose parents had divorced. The son was very angry with his father, and would not speak to him. He cooled off enough that a few years later, he invited his father to his high school graduation. When I went to greet him, his new wife introduced herself as "Johnny's other mom." "Johnny had never spoken to her!

If the new stepmom wants to have a good relationship with the child, they will allow the father to continue calling the shots on discipline. All feelings of jealousy of the children should be replaced with admiration of a dad who has maintained communication and affection with his offspring. Any disagreement between the two should be done in private. The child needs to see the two parents in unity. Some new stepmoms go out of their way to show they are in charge- this is foolish. This is particularly important if the biological mother is still in the picture.

b. Stepfathers

I have seen a few men who were amazing stepfathers. They had great relationships with both their genders. There were certain similar dynamics visible in each of these situations:

- Each was an active church goer

  These men were not only leading their families to God's House, they were involved to some extent in the church- greeting, cooking for events, ushering, etc. These children saw the man in their house in active in the House of God.

- Each spent large amounts of time with the stepchildren

  The men who succeeded in their roles in the blended families were at almost every game their stepdaughter or son played in. They planned weekend outings that the children enjoyed. They cheered often, criticized rarely or never. They were "over the top" in the support category- and that was okay with the kids! The biological parent to which each was married saw in their new life partner someone who could be counted on to support their child's dreams and aspirations. Of course, this increases the respect the natural mother has for this blended father.

These men lost sleep going on youth campouts, drove to games hours away, hosted events at the house, and were willing to pull out their wallets if the child needed/ wanted a snack or treat.

- They never insisted on being called, "Dad."

The most often way these dads were addressed was "Mr. _____". It was important to let the child choose the speed of the relationship, as much as the adults want to speed everything up. Eventually I was privileged to see this change in time to being called, "Dad."

- They were optimistic

You may have caught on to this from what I said previously. These guys were upbeat, funny (so sometimes the kids thought they were corny, that's endearing if handled well), and talked of how things were going to get better.

c. Blended Children

If you are in a circumstance where each of the couple is bringing in their own children to be blended under the same roof, you have a job cut out for you! Here are a few suggestions:

- Don't force them to be brothers and sisters.

Telling them by royal decree they are now brothers and sisters is lighting a fuse. The children are not stupid- they know they are stepsiblings. As I have said in each of these new roles, you cannot force emotions and feelings in someone else.

- Set the same boundaries for all the children

  If the children see the rules are consistent on both parties, they will handle the situation better. It is fine to make allowances and more privileges for the older children- everyone gets that. As long as it is explained, and they are told that when they are older they will have the same opportunities, most children will see this as reasonable.

- When possible, attempt to be the main parent for the child that is not yours. This is in non-threatening situations, such as pairing up on a ride or event.

"No Grace, this year you are only playing three sports."

-Grace's parents

# CHAPTER ELEVEN:

# TEAMING WITH OTHER PARENTS

*"Though one may be overpowered by another, **two** can withstand him. And a **three**fold cord is not quickly broken."* Eccl. 4:12

One of the great joys in raising our children is joining with like-minded couples in strategizing, sharing stories, victories ("Paul used the potty twice today!"), and concerns. It is almost impossible for humorous events not to occur in the interaction of families.

One among many episodes was when my wife and I went to another family's home for supper. We were visiting, but frankly the other couple looked exhausted. They were sitting- actually slouching- on their sofa, eyes drooping, and the body language could not have been clearer. Their offspring, on the other hand, were running, chasing each other, and laughing. It was at that point we felt we should say our goodbyes. Our hosts explained that their children were worn out; thus their behavior. Yeah, I do not think the children were the fatigued ones!

It is awesome for our sons and daughters to grow up interacting with another set of adults who say the same thing their parents say, place value on similar behaviors and virtues. The children see others their age being given the same boundaries (which has been discussed elsewhere in this volume). Vacationing together is a blast! While there should always be some vacations centered upon our family being alone, going with other families of similar vision was a highlight for our progeny growing up.

Sometimes we discover that the family we were close to prior to having children is on a different page than us regarding child-rearing. If this occurs it does not mean we cannot socialize, but it may be necessary to find other, like-minded families to with whom to connect.

A trap that we can fall into is wanting someone facing the same struggle we are having with our children or spouse and commiserating endlessly about our trials. While the saying "misery loves company" is certainly true, this is not the way to achieve victory in the situation. What is needed is not a "Jonathan" to our "David," but a "Paul" to our "Timothy." This means rather than finding someone else having rebellion problems, or marriage struggles, I would be better served finding someone who got through those crises and is now living in victory. There are older saints in the church who have been through far more than we have. These believers obtained great wisdom, gained through prayer and tears, and can often show us insights to get us through the trial. At the least they will usually add us to their prayer list.

# CHAPTER TWELVE:

## CULTURE WARS AND YOUR CHILDREN

*"Not until I went into the churches of America and heard her pulpits flame with righteousness did I understand the secret of her genius and power.*

*America is great because America is good, and if America ever ceases to be good, America will cease to be great.*

*The safeguard of morality is religion, and morality is the best security of law as well as the surest pledge of freedom."*

- Alexis de Tocqueville

*"If we ever forget that we are one nation under God, then we will be a nation gone under."*-Ronald Reagan

At the time of this writing, there are so many cultural flashpoints it is difficult to decide how many to discuss. It is very important for our teenagers to have a thought-out perspective on the issues that divide our nation along cultural lines. We should never be afraid of intellectual discussions on today's issues- the Scripture can hold it's own, and so can God's people!

What we are delving into is the study of Apologetics. According to the dictionary, apologetics is "the branch of theology concerned with the defense or proof of Christianity."

Charles Colson has discerned the situation correctly: *"If our culture is to be transformed, it will happen from the bottom up - from ordinary believers practicing apologetics over the backyard fence or around the barbecue grill."*

Our children must not first encounter the culture wars in college. This is the equivalent of sending someone into war without weapons or knowledge of defending oneself. One thing we must never say to our children is, "Don't think; just believe." If you have an intelligent child, this is almost a guaranteed way of losing them spiritually. Rather, join the child in researching the topic. Chuck Colson, again:

> "It's no understatement that the church has done a poor job in teaching our young people that reason and faith are not opposites, and that atheists are far from being on the side of reason. You can find on our website a chart which I use to demonstrate the various worldviews work out, and which one, Christianity, is rational. Many kids, however, who grow up huddled in a Christian **environment** find themselves in the university setting completely unequipped to defend the rationality of the Christian faith against the secular humanist worldview so prevalent on college campuses."

I am now going to give my view on dealing with society's battles that may offend some of you. I sincerely hope not, but I truly feel I am right on this, and after teaching thousands of teens I am convinced this is the right way to proceed in training our children.

It is not enough to prepare your children to debate the Christian position on abortion, homosexuality, extreme environmentalism, sex before marriage, and other pressure points in society by simply saying, "The Bible says so." If we are interested in standing up to a secular person's views, we must make the case outside of quoting scripture. This is not as difficult as you might think. If we are upholding a biblical view, the opposite should lead to negative outcomes. By diligently gathering the pertinent data, we can show a rational person that following the Scripture is better for society.

Let's take what at the time of this writing is a hot topic: homosexuality. I have taught in Bible class for years that when they mapped out the human genome, there would be no discovery of a "homosexual gene." If there were, then God would have created someone with a "sin" gene. The human genome has been mapped, and if there had been a homosexual gene, it would have been a three-inch headline in every major newspaper in the country. The fact we never saw such a headline is confirmation that, at least genetically, homosexuals are not born that way.

But what if it is eventually proven that people are predisposed to being gay? What then? Well, let's look at that possibility. Healthy teens are told that God's laws call for them to refrain from sexual intercourse until marriage. In their teens, children are biologically mature, meaning they are able to reproduce. So, God is asking of them to stand against something their body physically wants. How then, is a standard of calling for someone "born homosexual" to abstain from intercourse any different? Both want a physical satisfaction, both are being told to deny themselves. Thus the standard is not different than for a heterosexual who is not or never marries.

Going further, homosexuality can be opposed as to its effect on the fabric of society. From the Colson Center website:

American society is in the midst of a major debate over so-called same sex marriage. Those who argue for recognizing homosexual unions as marriage frame it as a civil rights issue and argue we don't have the right to impose our religious views of marriage on the rest of society.

They also frequently point out examples of celebrity divorces and serial marriages to argue that the state of marriage is so bad that allowing committed homosexuals to marry could hardly make matters worse.

At this point, it is worth looking into what marriage is and why it has been given a privileged place in all societies in human history. When I ask the students in my college classes this question, I have yet to get an answer: the students are largely clueless about what marriage is about in cross-cultural terms. To answer the question, we need to begin with sexuality. All societies view sexual activity as a moral issue even though the specific norms concerning sexual expression vary. The reason is simple: sexual activity can lead to pregnancy.

Childbearing is vitally important for society, since the future depends on the next generation. At the same time, social stability depends on maintaining some restrictions on childbearing: all societies have rules about who can reproduce with whom, and under what circumstances. They also have provisions for how the children are to be raised to become functioning members of society.

To provide a stable environment to bring children into the world and to raise them, societies recognize marriage, an institution whose basic function is to tie fathers and mothers to each other and to their children. This is essential for societal survival, and so marriages are recognized by the community and accorded special status.

The connection to childbearing means that marriage has always been a heterosexual institution; it varies in form, but the one constant is that it is heterosexual. Even in cultures that accept polygamy, the husband is married to each of the wives; the wives are not married to each other.

At this point, the objection that is regularly raised is that some couples cannot or do not wish to have children; does that make their marriages invalid? No, it doesn't. Think about it like this: legs are made for walking; the fact that some people cannot walk or choose not to does not mean we amputate their legs, nor does it invalidate the connection between legs and walking. In the same way, couples that do not have children do not change the fundamental function of marriage in society. In fact, the only reason why marriage is publicly recognized rather than simply a private arrangement is that it performs a public function related to childbearing and childrearing.

This does not mean that children are never born out of wedlock in traditional societies, of course. In most cases, however, these children, even if acknowledged by the father, do not have all the rights and privileges of children born in wedlock. Societies tend to attach a degree of stigma to them through no fault of their own, because they are the product of sexual activity outside the prescribed boundaries that promote a stable social order.

Of course, this is not the only means to support traditional marriage and attack the homosexual movement's narrative. It does, however, cause one to think how about social revolutions in terms secular people can understand. Of course, it is not our desire to attack or persecute homosexuals. God loves gays as well as straights.

But Homosexuality is a banned practice in Scripture, despite the exegetical contortions some have attempted to explain away the plain meaning of the Scriptures relative to the topic.

In no way am I backing down from citing Scripture as authoritative. We are seeing, rather, how to prepare our children to deal with arguments in the high schools and colleges where they may attend and be confronted for their views.

# CHAPTER THIRTEEN:

# ENVIRONMENTALISM

From TV cartoons to indoctrination in education, children have been trained to care a great deal about the planet and their environment. The water we drink, the air we breathe, and the other life forms on the earth have been deemed extremely important to their lives, along with the responsibility each has to guard and improve ecosystems which they inhabit.

Some rail against this, proclaiming it "Gaia Worship." Others are not sure how to handle this. Who wants to root for dirty air? Polluted rivers? Animals killed from contamination?

As Christians, we follow the biblical command given to all men from God to Adam, to rule over the earth. Ruling is not destroying, but looking after, tending, and protecting. This is what good rulers do. As Christians, we have a responsibility to care for the earth, as good stewards. Telling this to our offspring will create a bridge we can cross into their value system. At the same time, we can explain excesses that are promoted by an assortment of radical environmentalists, constantly proclaiming the end of life as we know it due to global cooling, global warming, air pollution in the U. S., (look at a satellite image of the earth, and see where the massive pollution is occurring. Then look at the U.S.- We are not the problem here.), or whatever the crisis du jour.

Okay, the fact is most of us feel overwhelmed attempting to train our kids in how to think about society's hot buttons. We might not have ever considered any of this ourselves! That means we need to either start getting educated, or put our children with people we trust who can prepare them for what lies ahead. A sharp pastor on staff might be the answer, or a quality Christian school teacher.

# CHAPTER FOURTEEN:

## DATING

Brother: "Hey dad, I got a girlfriend."
Dad: "Good job, son!"

Sister: "Hey, daddy, I got a boyfriend."
Dad: (Loads shotgun)

Dating

My half serious rule when my children were young was they could date when they were 21, and then only in groups of 16 or more. When the bus came around, they could board it.

I distinctly remember when my wife and oldest daughter no longer thought this was funny. My daughter liked a boy, and was seriously wanting to know when she could date.

When she was 14, a nice Christian boy came to my office at the church and asked if he could start dating my daughter. Of course, I said "No." He asked if I was serious, and I informed him I had never been more serious in my life. When he asked why, I told him it wasn't personal. There was no one who could have come into that door and received a "Yes." (By the way, she is now married to this young man of God, and at the time of this writing they are youth pastors of a very large youth group in a major city in the U.S.

Everyone wants a hard answer to when his or her child should begin dating. That way, the parents have someone to blame. "I'm sorry, honey. I really think he's nice and would be fine with you going out. But that book we got says you cannot, so too bad."

In our home, the rule was dating started at the beginning of the senior year. Let me explain how we arrived at this rule. We believe the young lady or man is simply too immature to be in a serious relationship before that age. Does that mean there are no mature children in this sphere prior to that? Not necessarily, but in a home whatever rule you use will be brought with the next child in line.

Not everyone agreed with us on this. I remember a friend of our daughter had a mom who wanted her daughter dating at the ripe old age of 12. My oldest was invited to go bowling with two other girls. I said that was fine. Later I discovered this was  the mom arranging for the three girls to meet three junior high boys at the bowling alley. Imagine their surprise when the young men arrived. I could smell them almost before I could see them. Hair blown, enough cologne to cause an allergic reaction. Coming to meet three cute girls. Probably already having selected who each would pursue. Only one problem. I was there, the principal of their school, the dad of one of the girls, and the uninvited party crasher! Making a long story short, the boys chose to bowl on another lane, and for some reason did not associate with the girls. Of course, you are wondering how my mortified daughter handled this. The therapist says she will probably be okay by age 30.

Dating is an expected part of the teen years, and in many cases, the preteen years. I believe this is a ticking time bomb, and this is one of the hills as parents we must be willing to die on. I am not going to give you a threshold age your child should be allowed to start dating. There are many factors related to maturity and the crowd with which your child hangs out. What I do wish to do is give you factors to consider when deciding the appropriate age for dating in your family:

1. What age you set for your responsible, clear-headed oldest is going to be for your "push the limits" younger child.

2. Is the first step going to be group dates, double dates, or single dating? Are you willing to enforce it?

3. Would you or your spouse have been responsible to go out with another person's child when you were that age? What, do you think your offspring is far more mature than you were at that age? Why?

4. What constitutes a "date"? Going to the show? Meeting at a ball game? You better be able to handle this like a lawyer,

because I assure you your child will be when you address the topic of dating.

5. How far are you willing to go in giving your child's date the third degree regarding their family background, spending time with you- the dad- before your daughter walks out the door?

6. Are you and your spouse going to stick to your guns when crunch time comes? It's easy to say what the boundaries will be when they are in lower elementary. But can your son or daughter bend you when they first get asked out, or want to ask someone else out?

7. Are you going to set different ages for your children based on gender? Responsibility and maturity? (Good luck)

8. Have you discussed curfews? (This will be the subject of another section in this book)

9. Have you chosen your favorite weapon in case things don't turn out well? (Okay, this was a joke, sort of)

10. Do you have the kind of relationship with your child where they feel they     can discuss with you how the relationship is going? (hint: you cannot answer     this nearly as well as your child can)

# CHAPTER FIFTEEN:

# SINGLE PARENTING

"I didn't set out to be a single parent. I set out to be the best parent I can be... and that hasn't changed."
- OneMomsGuide.com

## Single Parenting

The quote on the last page pretty much sums up many single parents' mindset. Few chose single parenthood as their first option, but what can be done to help the child grow well adjusted and complete?

The first observation I would like to make is referenced earlier in this book. Mothers should not take the role of correction and discipline in their sons' lives as they grow into their later teen years. The mother's role in the son's life is one of encouragement and nurturing, whereas the father's role is one of discipline and training. Particularly for single moms with sons, it is critical that someone is in the "disciplining and training" mode. How is this to take place?

Unless there is an active grandfather or uncle to take the position of father, the local church must fill this role. I cannot emphasize the need for the position to be filled. If the local church does not provide some avenue to address this need, another ministry might be necessary.

In the elementary years, the children's pastor would be a great place to start. Involving your child in the life of the children's ministry at every juncture will give the children's pastor the opening to develop a quality relationship with your child. It is critical the man know the situation, and what your wanting for your child. Set up an appointment to address this. Regular meetings with the leader should be available. Remember the woman and the unjust judge (Lk. 18:1-5). *"You have not because you have not."* Is also still in Scripture.

**Teens**

A few years ago, a young man came to the office to set up an appointment with me. He told the counselor he needed to talk to me "man to man." Sounds promising, right? I thought so, too, until the counselor informed me he had a classmate come with him because he was anxious about talking to the guidance counselor!

Raising teens to serve the Lord is difficult! Doing it as a single mom or dad can seem impossible! Again, a godly male in the immediate family is ideal for helping the single mom, and likewise a godly woman in the family for the single dad.  The youth group leaders should be available to fill these roles if there is no one else. They are young enough to relate to the teen, and hopefully wise enough to give sound counsel. When you tell your child they are making an unwise choice of friends, or dating someone they shouldn't, it often does not connect. When the Youth Pastor or his wife (I really hope your youth pastor is married) talk to them, they will often listen more readily. Again, scheduling an appointment for yourself with the youth ministry is a great means of explaining the type of assistance you are requesting and a discussion of a game plan and how to implement that plan.

# CHAPTER SIXTEEN:

# DEALING WITH INSECURITES IN CHILDREN

"The reason we struggle with insecurity is because we compare out behind-the-scenes with everyone else's highlight reel."
- Steve Furtick

## Dealing with insecurities in our children

Contrary to what one would assume, the prisons are full of people who have great self-esteem. In and of itself, self-esteem is not a panacea for all ills. But self-esteem connected to God is a great thing, and vital to our children's making it through life. Many of our children deal with insecurity. They wonder if they are smart enough, pretty enough, tough enough, good enough, to be successful in their eyes, your eyes, and most all in their friends' eyes. Simply put, it is not possible to tell your children often enough that with God's help they can accomplish whatever God's plan for them includes.

The key here is that our self-esteem is rooted in being created by God. As C.S. Lewis says repeatedly in <u>The Chronicles of Narnia,</u> we are "sons of Adam and daughters of Eve." Lewis speaking through the character, Aslan, says it better than I could:

> *"I was wishing that I came of a more honourable lineage."*
>
> *"You come of the Lord Adam and the Lady Eve," said Aslan." "And that is both honour enough to erect the head of the poorest beggar, and shame enough to bow the shoulders of the greatest emperor on earth. Be content."*

The pastor, Chris Hodges, preaches that he used Tigger as his children's role model. When they had to tackle something new, they were to take the attitude, "That's what I do best." Okay, that's not totally realistic, but a "can do" attitude is certainly better than a "this won't work" ethic.

Some parents critique everything their child does, pointing out their errors. With some children this will develop a hatred of the activity, to the point they will search for something to be involved in apart from their parents, and that can never be good.

As I mentioned under the blended families segment, dads need to tell their daughters how beautiful they are, and how proud they are of their children. **Your love must be unconditional.** You love your child because they are your child; not because of their success. If a child feels loved conditionally, whether justified or not, they will either live their life trying to always be good enough (no, that is a very bad thing), or they will surrender and seek unconditional love elsewhere. All of our children did well in their elementary and secondary education, and some were recognized in athletics. None of this was a basis for our devotion to our children, and they knew it.

# CHAPTER SEVENTEEN:

## PK'S AND TK'S

(Preachers' kids and teachers' kids) Yeah, they need their own section

"Why are preachers' kids so bad? Because they have to play with the deacons' kids."
- very old joke

PKs and TKs

Preachers' kids and to a lesser extent, teachers' kids, live in a world a little different from everyone else. They live with the knowledge any mistake they make, any sin and most careless mistakes, can and will be used against <u>their parents</u> in the court of public opinion. The responsibility is great on the pastor and teacher parents not to put more pressure on their child to live a sinless life. (Which is pretty hard. In fact I seem to remember something in Romans 3 about no one being able to do it.)

The pastor and teacher must absolutely refuse to allow this to happen. The attacks against their children, and their own parenting as a natural consequence, must be dealt with on absolute terms. "My child is not your concern. I am his/ her parent, and will discipline when and how I see fit." For more ammunition, you could point out what I have found to be a nearly universal truth: Folks don't pray for people they talk about, and they don't talk about people they really pray for.

If you think being a preacher's kid is no different from any other type of child, take a look at these from http://pkn.ag.org/you-know-youre-a-pk-when/
1. You think the definition of the word fellowship involves food.

2. People constantly tell you that they changed your diapers in the nursery or remember when you were "this big!"

3. You learned how to answer every Sunday school question by the age of four with three simple words: "God? Jesus? Bible?"

4. Family vacation meant a Preacher's conference.

5. You keep an extra set of clothes at the church just in case.

6. You love playing hide and go seek in the dark in the sanctuary.

7. People in the congregation turn and smile at you or look for some reaction when your dad gets loud or makes a stupid joke.

8. Your family gets a lifetime supply of banana bread, and you end up eating it even though you don't like it.

9. You know that for every bible story, there is a VeggieTales movie.

10. People always ask you for a key for something

11. You can become an illustration in a sermon without a moments notice or any consent forms signed.

12. You know who the unmentionable names are in sermon stories.

13. Everyone knows who you are but you may never know their name.

14. Your name is often substituted with "_____ daughter/son"

15. You know every hiding spot in the church.

16. You have put in hours of waiting for your parents to stop talking or lock up

17. You know who gives out candy in the church and where to find it in the Pastor's office.

18. You volunteer in EVERY area of the church.

19. You are sick on Sunday, and your parents tell you to "throw up and prove it". When you do, they say, "Now don't you feel better? Let's go to church!"

20. Singing in church was your first exposure to "performing".

We thought we'd bring back this fun post! Can anyone add any more?

Here is a great insight from a pastor who knows:

**From http://nagsheader.blogspot.com/2008/04/what -you-might-not-know-about-your_05.html**

## What you might not know about your pastor's kids

I know about pastor's kids. Growing up, I was often friends with my pastors' kids and spent time in their homes. During my college years my own dad entered the pastorate, so while I'm not a pastor's kid, my youngest two brothers went through adolescence in a pastor's home. And of course my own children have for most of their lives been pastor's children. So I am somewhat of an expert, for what it's worth.

Pastors' kids are kids. Like their moms, they didn't receive a call from God to their lot in life growing up. So they have no choice in the matter. But, you might say, neither do any children. Kids don't determine what their parents do career-wise. Yeah, but most careers don't put their children in a fishbowl, either.

They don't want to be looked at differently. They just want to be treated as normal kids like everyone else's. That shouldn't be too hard. But for some reason in many churches it is.

They aren't perfect, so don't expect them to be. Hey, they're just like your kids. You've heard the joke. Why are preachers kids so bad? Because they play with the deacons' kids.

Unless they are your children they're not yours to discipline. And if you do see them truly misbehave, tell it to their parents, not to other church members or to "the board". It's not their business. Give them the same respect you expect. Take them out from under the microscope.

In many cases they likely carry some resentment toward the church because of a number of things. Typically...

- Dad can't attend their ballgames/dance recitals/camping trips, etc. because he has to take care of the church. Yet other church members have no problem attending their kids functions. Kids aren't stupid. They see the inconsistencies and unfairness.

- They have to attend church every time the doors are open. Sometimes because "we have to set the example". But they don't want to be the examples. They want to be normal. Remember, it's not their "calling".

- They hear the criticisms of their dad. This one really stinks. No kid should hear another adult or hear of another adult blasting their parents, even if the criticism is warranted. But it happens way too often in churches. Adults can handle that stuff. Kids shouldn't have to.
- They see the stress at home that balancing ministry and family causes his parents and their relationship. Again, pastoring is a 24/7 job. See my previous posts on this subject. In most cases (I say most because I talk to lots of pastors across this country) their father is overworked and underpaid. So they don't have the income to take the nice vacation or buy the better clothes or get the latest gadgets for Christmas. Sorry, but it's true.

That's enough. You get the picture.

Just because dad's a pastor doesn't mean they want to be one. In fact, depending on how the church treats their dad will largely determine their relationship with the church as an adult. Just because dad's a pastor doesn't mean they are believers. And if they aren't, they have to put on the act. And that makes them dislike themselves because they know they're pretending. Treat them like any other child who needs Christ – with love.

If you give them their space and privacy they'll like you a whole lot more. And they'll like the church, too. If they don't feel like oddballs because dad's a pastor, they could turn out normal.

Most pastors kids are genuinely caring children who want both to please their parents and their God. They're not super-spiritual, but can be spiritually dynamic people if they get the same chances to just be kids like everyone else. There are some great success stories of pastor's children who go on to accomplish wonderful things in life through whatever careers they choose. But because they are who they are, so much is made or broken by how dad's church(es) treat them and their parents.

Having said all that I think my three children (and they're free to respond here) have no regrets from being reared in a pastor's home. They're all three healthy and committed to their families and are all active in their churches. My son is a full-time worship leader working with me. My first daughter married a youth pastor and is in another state. My youngest daughter and her husband are nearby and are great volunteers in our church. I'm not bragging- just saying being a pastor's kid doesn't have to be negative or stressful. But I also give my church credit for allowing my family to just be a family, and for praying for us over the years.

- Rick Lawrenson

Thom Rainier found these responses from preachers' kids:

1. **The glass house is a reality.** People are always looking at the PKs. They have trouble saying or doing anything without someone, usually a church member, making a comment. Most of these PKs (and former PKs) felt a great deal of discomfort living in the glass house. Some even expressed bitterness.

2. **Some church members made a positive and lasting impression on PKs.** One of the more frequent positive comments we heard were about the church members who loved and cared for the PKs. Many of them took the children under the wings and made a positive difference in their lives.

3. **Some church members were jerks to the PKs.** Many of the stories are heartbreaking. It is really hard to imagine some of the awful

words that were said to the PKs. Some still feel the sting of those words decades later.

4. **Many PKs resent the interrupted meals and vacations.** They felt like their pastor parent put the church before the family. One PK, now an adult, lamented that every vacation his family took was interrupted; and many times the vacation was truncated.

5. **Some of the PKs have very positive memories when their parents included them in the ministry.** I read comments about hospital visits, nursing home visits, and ministry in the community. These PKs absolutely loved doing ministry with mom and dad. They felt like the church ministry was something the whole family did.

6. **A key cry from the PKs was: "Let me be a regular kid."** A number of the PKs expressed pain from the high expectations placed upon them by both their parents and church members. Others said that some church

members expected them to behave badly because that's just what PKs do.

7. **Some PKs left the church for good because of their negative experiences.** They viewed local congregations as a place for judgmental Christians who are the worst of hypocrites. They have no desire ever to return. You can feel the resentment and pain in their comments. Their hurt is palpable.

# CHAPTER EIGHTEEN:

# PRODIGALS

"I believe God created teenagers to punish us so we would know what it felt like to have someone created in our own image that denied our existence."

- Jeff Allen

**Prodigals**

So many sermons have been preached on the Prodigal Son and the variations (the attitude of the older brother, etc.) that I hesitated to include a section on this. But reflecting on the sermons I heard, I did not really remember much being said about how to handle the prodigal *while they are still prodigals.* I thought I would give some perspectives on this.

## Unconditional Love

We are called to love the prodigal. I am not referring to some emotional tug, but an act of the will that is shown first by not ceasing to pray for him or her. Unconditional love is shown by desiring God's goals for all our relationships, including the prodigal son or daughter. These goals include:

Matt. 5:42-44
- Giving to whoever asks
- Bringing healing in any and all areas

Matt. 25:34-40
- Feeding the hungry
- Clothing the naked
- Visiting the sick and imprisoned

Phil. 2:5
- Having the same attitude as Christ

## Motivation

Our motivation for reaching out to the prodigal and offering help must be examined. If we are doing it out of intimidation, fear, or guilt then we are not serving Christ, but emotional blackmail. The Boundaries series by Dr. Henry Cloud and John Townsend give a great explanation in detail regarding this area.

## Selfless Service to the Prodigal?

We saw earlier our goals as Christians toward the prodigal son or daughter are the same as toward anyone else. But with those goals the Scripture has placed checks and balances. Here are a few of Jesus' teachings and the scriptural boundary:

- **"Feed the hungry."** Yes, but *"If anyone will not work, neither let him eat."* II Thess. 3:10

- **"Love everyone."** *"If people are causing divisions among you, give a first and second* warning. *After that, have nothing more to do with them.*" Titus 3:10 Note, we can and should love them and pray for them. But we are not required by God to put up with their strife and turmoil. Indeed, we are commanded not to allow it to bring disunity!

- "**Forgive anyone who sins against you**." This one is absolute. We are not to hold any sin against the person who commits it. We are to forgive and pray God's blessings on their life. **But this is not saying we should continue to be placed in circumstances where it will occur repeatedly.** Look at Matt. 18:15-17 How are we to treat pagans and tax collectors? Loving and praying for them to be saved. (c.f. II Thess. 3:14-15)

## Allowing the Principle of Sowing and Reaping to Work the Work of God

A great principle of scripture is sowing and reaping, or planting and harvesting. **Gal. 6:7** This principle was established by God so we would receive the results of our actions, whether good or bad. **We frustrate the laws of God when we enable the person not to learn God's lessons.**

Am I Helping or Hurting?

The question of how much to aid the prodigal son or daughter while they are still wayward is this: Am I helping them or merely enabling their wrong attitudes and behaviors to continue. I will answer the question: Are they getting better? If not, I am enabling, not helping.

So Do I Invite Them Over?

I believe the prodigal child should be included in any family events going on, as long as their behavior does not violate the values of your family. This is particularly so if there are still minors in the house who could be affected (infected?). If the prodigal is living in sin, and you cannot insure their behavior in your home, you might be better served inviting them to activities in neutral places- a restaurant, etc.

Prodigals Who Are Dysfunctional
Cloud and Townsend identify several types of dysfunctional people who I am relating to prodigals. I've included some of these and what the scripture would say about each:

- **Anger issues- Pr. 19:19** *"Hot-tempered people must pay the penalty. If you rescue them once you will have to do it again."* The idea we must excuse or bail out these persons just allows it to happen more. You may have one of these in your home. You are not required to watch the show. Tell them to call you when they are better. Often without an audience, the explosion is shorter.

- **People with no control**. As with the others in our group, these can be in addictions. Rom. 7:15-23 describes them well. In v. 25 we find the only answer: *"Thank God! The answer is in Jesus Christ our Lord."*

- **"Drainers"** These are the individuals who need other people's attention. Their need is insatiable. The problem is they need a relationship with the heavenly Father, who alone can meet every need. Neither you nor anyone else in his or her world can meet all their need for attention. **It is especially important to recognize this if you are a "mercy" person!**

- **Manipulators**- this can be found in the others mentioned, but they will use bullying, guilt, and will often attempt to isolate us from others so they can have us for themselves.

How Should We Pray For Prodigals?

1. Pray with assurance- Jesus loves them more than you do. "*Will not the judge of all the earth do right?*"

2. Pray without ceasing- the battle is not over until we give up or win.

3. Pray the scriptures- you can often find Psalms to fit the situation you are dealing in.

# CHAPTER NINETEEN:

# THE ROLE OF EDUCATION IN RAISING GODLY KIDS

"I am afraid that the schools will prove the very gates of hell, unless they diligently labor in explaining the Holy Scriptures and engraving them in the heart of the youth."

- Martin Luther

## The Role of Education in Raising Godly Kids

Children spend the majority of the year in school about 8 hours per day. In fact, they are with the teachers and fellow students far more waking hours each week than they are with their parents. What are the goals and outcomes desired from the education process?

## Choices

There are basically three options for a child's education. They are public school, private/parochial school, and home school. Questions abound on the part of parents regarding each:

- Are my children going to be okay in public school? What if it is considered a quality school?

- What about Christian schools? Are they all alike? What should I be looking for; what questions to ask?

- I've heard some people tell me homeschooling is the way to go. I wouldn't know where to start! Is this a viable option?

## The Public School

Most churches have at least a few members who teach or who have taught in the public school system. These are people who have tried to make a difference in the lives of the children. They are to be honored for their service. In many cases their labor has been that of the missionary. I taught for several years in public school elementary and secondary education. My parents each taught for decades in both public and parochial schools. It is from these experiences, as well as what is occurring in the news daily, that I make some observations.

The public school setting is designed to teach information a child needs to be productive in their later lives. Obviously some do this better than others. What is not in the design of the public school is to inculcate biblical values. The values children are exposed to center around the one great value of Tolerance. In fact, this is about the only value that is given much credence. Since Tolerance is the most important value in the belief system of public schools in the United States, any concept of absolutes, or "Rights and Wrongs," must be surrendered. To the idea that one should never steal, the response is, "What were the circumstances? Maybe they were doing the best they could." No behavior in and of itself is wrong. Each person is allowed their own value system, and all are equal. This is a main cause for so few Christians in the U.S. holding that there are absolutes in ethics.

## IF YOUR PRE-K CHILD IS NOT READY TO ADVANCE

"*Welcome to Lake Wobegon, where all the women are strong, all the men are good-looking, and* ***all the children are above average.***"

(This probably does not belong in this book, but it keeps coming up in my work as a principal, and I would hate for a christian family to be getting things going right spiritually only to have a mistake happen in their five year old that would impair his or her development, so I am throwing this in as "lagniappe.")

When one of our children was five years old, we brought him in for Kindergarten screening. He seemed very bright in some areas, but physically limited in fine motor skills. He had some medical issues when younger that had impeded development.

We were heart broken when he was judged not to be ready to go into the class his age dictated, i.e., Kindergarten. As things turned out, during the summer we moved, and when we enrolled our children in the new school, they evaluated our five year old and determined he was, in fact, ready to enroll. But what if he had not been?

I strongly urge any parent to understand that children can be educationally young. This means a child might be more successful in a younger class age wise. When looking at a chart of child development, it appears as a smooth incline. The fact is the individual child develops more like stairs-jumps in progress, then a plateau, followed by another jump.

The parents who have taken our advice to stay with the younger class level have been rewarded with seeing their children successful in later years of school. This increases the potential for a happy, fruitful educational experience for the student.

Let's look at the alternative: if the child keeps moving up based on age, they could reach a point where they are so far behind that they cannot grow academically. Let's say this occurs (as I have often seen it) in third grade. The problem is it is too late to go back to first, where the child would be one of the strongest academic students. Rather, they will stay in third until they are barely able to pass, then of course they will be advanced to fourth, where, again they will be among the weakest students. This will likely result in a child who dislikes school, and feels inferior to the other children.

The push back against my position on this is the resentment that the child is being considered "too stupid to go to kindergarten." This is not the case at all. Rather, it is placing the child in best position to be successful, like school, and find their place in society without being short-circuited at an early age.

# CHAPTER TWENTY:

## "Okay, I Get It. But My Child is 14- How Do I Begin From Here?"

A young couple came up to me recently with a version of the question above. They had no background in Scripture or church, and their eyes had been open. But their child was pushing back hard on the changes they were attempting to bring into their homes and personal lives. Boundaries were being set up for which the child had no point of reference. How does a family go from being carried along by the current of the culture to "swimming upstream" against the movement further and further from God's ways as taught in Scripture?

I would not encourage a heavy-handed dictatorial approach. Often this is the method of new Christian parents. I believe some of this is the uncertainty of what to do, and the pressure makes us pull into a "Because I said so" approach. As I will explain in a moment, this was my experience as an 18 year old living at home when my parents came to a new revelation of the Lord Jesus Christ.

The first thing that must change is us!

We as parents must be willing to lay ourselves open before the Lord and ask Him to show us the areas **we have failed** to live as examples for our children. This is not to wallow in regret, but to lay a foundation for the future. Repentance before the Lord is a key to God's blessings. This is why David said in Ps. 51, "Against Thee only have I sinned."

This would include:

- Repenting for our lack of godly wisdom and direction to our children. We must ask their forgiveness for the lateness of our awakening, and explain that we are beginning anew (II Cor. 5:17).
- Repenting for sowing seeds of criticism and harshness ("Provoke not your children to wrath.")

- Failing to break off generational curses (covered earlier)

   Next, there must be multiple meetings with our teens explaining not only what is changing, but why.
The Family Pastor, or Life Pastor, or even a more knowledgeable married couple, is invaluable in coaching us through these meetings.    Some topics might include:

- Why shows we used to watch are no longer permitted.
- Why events and outings the family used to attend will no longer be part of the family plans
- Asking the child what bothers them about the changes, and what would they like you to do to help them over the transition.

   Obviously the goal is to have the children "buy in" to what we are telling them, but that may be a long process- particularly if they are strong-willed or rebellious. But this remains the goal, because our prayer is that they will adopt these precepts into their own families when they are grown.

**Some strategies to help with this process**:

- It's possible your child will think they are the only ones on the planet that have to do this. The more children of like-minded parents they spend time with, the less crazy it will seem

- Putting your child in the youth group will have another adult speaking into their life your new values.

- Getting your children into a Christian school might be an option.

- Get your child to Youth Camp, and pray for breakthroughs. Warn the youth pastor and staff if your child is pushing back against the idea of going.

- A major focus must be that we live what we say we now believe. One of the great teachers in Scripture, Ezra, "prepared his heart to seek the Law of the Lord, and to do it, and to teach statutes and ordinances in Israel." (Ez. 7:10) Prepare your heart, seek the Lord, do the works of God, and then teach them to your children.

We must remember that the God Who loved us and sent His Son loves our son or daughter more than we do!

If the child is almost out of high school, a somewhat different strategy will need to be in place. While the rules in the house are your call (that never changes), the realization that your child may soon leave your sphere of influence means a change in approach to introducing them to your attempt to live holy before the Lord. Respecting their freedom to make choices that to some extent are not what you would approve is part of the process of growing up. It can bring us to our knees as parents, but this is part of the transition from child to adult. When our children became seniors in high school, there was less their getting permission, and more letting us know what they were doing. We still maintain veto power, but it was rarely used. If your child is 17 or 18, they will determine what they think of all this "God business" by what they see in your lives. That's what happened in my life. We were "CEOs" at church: Christmas and Easter Only. When my parents became regular church goers- even on Wednesdays- I did not know what was going on. I came to understand, got hungry for what they had, and took off from there.

# Scripture Index:

www.ingramcontent.com/pod-product-compliance
Lightning Source LLC
LaVergne TN
LVHW051228080426
835513LV00016B/1477